Metamorphosis

Why Christians Don't Change

Dr. Michael E. Frisina

Printed in the United States of America

ISBN 978-1-60791-187-6

www.xulonpress.com

To Ginny & Carl:

Sue and I so cherish your friendship and your service to our Church family. May the Lord continue to richly bless you as you transform into the image of our Lord & Savior, Jesus Christ.

Blessings,
Michael

Romans 8:28-29

Contents

The butterfly, its wings having been strengthened by the struggle to exit the cocoon, gracefully emerged from its chrysalis and took flight, headed for "a world more loving and glorious than we can imagine."

D. Brookes Cowan, Ph.D., MSW

I am the butterfly. No more worm, out of the cocoon. I am the butterfly soaring on the wind that is the Lord. Made, remade and recreated by Him.

Carl W. Naso

The Cocoon & the Butterfly

A man found a cocoon of a butterfly. One day a small opening appeared. He sat and watched the butterfly for several hours as it struggled to force its body through that little hole. Then it seemed to stop making any progress. It appeared as if it had gotten as far as it had and it could go no further.

Then the man decided to help the butterfly, so he took a pair of scissors and snipped off the remaining bit of the cocoon. The butterfly then emerged easily. But it had a swollen body and small, shriveled wings. The man continued to watch the butterfly because he expected that, at any moment, the wings would enlarge and expand to be able to support the body, which would contract in time.

Neither happened! In fact, the butterfly spent the rest of its life crawling around with a swollen body and shriveled wings. It never was able to fly.

What the man in his kindness and haste did not understand was that the restricting cocoon and the struggle required for the butterfly to get through the tiny opening were God's way of forcing fluid from the body of the butterfly into its wings so that it would be ready for flight once it achieved its freedom from the cocoon.

Sometimes struggles are exactly what we need in our life. If God allowed us to go through our life without any obstacles, it would cripple us. We would not be as strong as what we could have been. And we could never fly.

(Author unknown)

Forward

My Metamorphous

Trembling and afraid, cold sweat on my body, ice in my stomach, and sweat in my palms; as long as I can remember, this was how I experienced life. It did not matter whether I was in gym class or math class when called upon to perform; this was my instinctive emotional response. You see, I believed that I could not do it. I could not perform to the expectations of others no matter what I was asked or required to do. I was convinced I was right. I could not, and so I did not. My behavior followed my thinking, and I lived a tormented miserable life.

I often wondered how others succeeded when I could not. I finally convinced myself I was doomed to failure. I quit trying to do anything well and put forth the minimum amount of effort just to get by. Consequently, I was labeled lazy, weak, and a person who could not "get it done." I lived trapped in this flawed self-image until I was twenty-five-years old.

At the age of twenty-five I finally snapped. My weight ballooned to almost three hundred pounds, and I was still living at home with my parents and playing with toy soldiers for fun - at the age of twenty- five! I was at the lowest point in my life when I decided to prove everyone else wrong about what they believed about me and what I believed about myself. I went back to college at night and in three years completed a bachelor's degree in business and graduated with honors. I lost fifty pounds and started training as a weight lifter. I also went to a local martial arts school and trained with one instructor in full contact mixed martial arts - boxing, kick- boxing, and grappling. I went from no social life to dating multiple women in a two year span. I was proving the world wrong on the outside, but inside I knew I had not changed what I believed to be true about me.

You see my motivator for change was fear. I was afraid of whom I really was deep down inside and that fear drove me to overcompensate in every aspect of my life. When the chips were down and I needed to get to my core, my foundation, deep down inside I still saw myself as weak and lazy and the guy who just could not "get it done." This false belief continued to guide my thoughts and behavior. When fighting on the mat against opponents in martial arts, I was not fighting to win but instead fighting to avoid getting injured. Consequently, I was injured three times in one year. When pulling a heavy dead lift or getting under a big squat, I did not intend to get hurt, yet I injured and re-injured myself several times. I now have two ruptured discs as physical scars from my flawed belief system. The saddest part of this whole story is that I was a born again Christian! I thought this misery was part of the Christian experience!

Then several years ago in my mid-thirties, I met Michael Frisina. He became a spiritual mentor and teacher, guiding me through the Word of God. During our time together, I came to learn the truth that what I believed determined what I thought, and what I thought determined how I lived my life. So with Michael's help, I began to develop self-awareness and the courage to examine the beliefs I had hidden in my heart. Doing this was painful but necessary to begin my transformation process.

I started reading the Bible with a passion and began believing what God said in His Word. Galatians 2:20 says, "I am crucified with Christ, it is no longer I who live but Christ who lives in me...." When I got to this verse, it all started to click. In God's Word, God Himself said that the old man is dead, and I am a new man. A new man in Jesus Christ is NOT lazy, weak, or an "I can't get it done" kind of guy. God said so!

Once I realized I had an unbiblical core belief system in my heart that was guiding my actions, I went to the Bible to see what God said about me. I then began to see myself in the light of God's Word. In Christ, I am a highly motivated, strong, fit, intelligent, passionate, charismatic, loving, and a fun loving person who can do all things through Christ Jesus who strengthens me! I am FEARLESS. I am not afraid of life or death! I look forward to Monday morning as much as I look forward to the weekend! I am FREE! I am enjoying and loving life like never before. I am the butterfly because of what I was taught, what I learned, what I understood, and because I applied a simple but profound concept: what I believe determines what I think, and what I think determines how I live!

Why should you read this book? If you are miserable inside and want to change but don't know how, this book is for you. If you want to live the abundant life God has called all of us as Christians to live, then this book is for you. Most of all, if you want to know and taste the absolute freedom of living a life of victory in Christ, this book is for you. I am not living a unique life but a life that God designed all of us to live as Christians.

John 8:36 says, "Therefore if the Son makes you free you shall be free indeed." The journey to true freedom in Christ starts with the next page. May you be bold and courageous enough to turn the page, and may you soar like the butterfly God created you to be!

Carl W. Naso
Associate Pastor, Calvary Chapel Northeast
Columbia

Preface

Common sense and a lot of research dictate that if you want to change the outcomes of your life and improve your performance in both your personal life and professional life, you have to learn how to manage yourself. Simply stated, you have to learn how to make more effective choices so you derive more effective outcomes and consequences from the choices you make. If your life is going to be more reflective of whom you want to be and what you desire to accomplish, then it is absolutely necessary for you to learn to close the gap between what you believe to be true and what you ultimately reveal in your chosen behavior.

This book will teach you what you need to learn about how to close the gap between what you say you believe to be true and how you actually behave. This book not only provides you a strategy to live your life in biblical alignment but also provides the specific "how-to" in daily actions and new habits. Direct observation of human behavior, particularly among those who claim to believe in God, His Son, salvation, redemption, and a host of other biblical truths, indicates a major inconsistency between what we say we believe and how we choose to behave. Why? Why is it within the so-called church we have such a difficult time *walking our talk* as they say?

Listen to critics and those outside the faith circle. What is the number one objection to believing God, His Word, the free gift of salvation, and joining a local church fellowship - in a word, hypocrites. Those on the outside, as Paul refers to unbelievers in his letter to the Thessalonians, see the gap between what we profess and how we behave. For those of us in the church, our typical response is that there are hypocrites at the mall and the grocery stores too. Our counter argument is to suggest that no one is perfect. Well I have news for you; the Bible says as Christians we ought to be perfect even as Christ is perfect (Matthew 5:48). If we really believed that the wages of sin is death, would we be more inclined to strive for the excellence in Christ that the apostle Paul wrote about to his missionary churches?

The purpose of this book is two fold. First to argue that as authentic Christians we are lazy and complacent in our walk in the Spirit. I know this might not be a very good marketing strategy for a book, but marketing is not my objective – you living an abundant life in Christ is my main goal. To accomplish that goal I need to be able to lovingly reveal the truth to you about basic human nature, and you have to be willing to accept that what I am telling you is true. Consequently, I believe as Christians we take a casual and cavalier approach to sin in our lives forgetting

Paul's exhortation that we are not to sin so that grace may abound. There is an active role and effort on our part to abstain from sin and fulfill the will of God in our lives as authentic believers – our sanctification (1Thess 4:3). You will never abound in the joy, peace, love, and contentment in your personal relationship with Jesus Christ until you can understand that your life in Christ is to be completely separate from the life in the flesh.

If you have a desire to walk in blessing and contentment, then you need to read this book. I will walk you through the transformation process from a life lived to satisfy your own desires to a life of service to the Lord Jesus Christ. The Bible gives us a mystery, a paradox – if we die in our Adam nature, then we will live in our Christ nature. We must die to live. That is what the Bible says. In this book you will learn what it means to die to self so you can walk consistently in behavior that keeps what you believe in alignment with how you choose to behave.

My desire for you in reading this book is that you will finally discover and be able to live an abundant Christian life. I am so tired of seeing people who claim to be authentic Christians walk around in defeat. Do you really believe that such behavior will win the lost to Christ? The purpose of this book is to answer the question about why Christians don't change. I want you to discover why so many Christians continue to struggle with lusts and desires that cripple and wound their witness for Christ. Every Sunday we pray for the Lord to deliver us from the web of sin. Well as one old fellow found out on a particular Sunday, we are praying the wrong prayer. Forget the web of sin; we need to pray for someone to kill the spider!

As you read this book, I want you to know that I have already prayed that the Lord would kill the spider in your life. I have already prayed for you that the eyes of your heart would be opened and that you would see with great conviction and clarity of purpose to choose to live your life based on what you believe to be true about God, the Bible, Jesus Christ, salvation, and the hope of your future glory in heaven. May the Lord truly bless you and set you free from the false beliefs that lead to destructive behaviors. May the Lord renew your heart and your mind so you may walk in the Spirit and receive all the blessings promised to you by the Word of God. May the Lord bless you and keep you, and may His face keep shining upon you.

Blessings to you, Michael

Introduction

*All changes, even the most longed for, have their
melancholy; for what we leave behind us is a part
of ourselves; we must die to one life before we can
enter another. ~Anatole France*

This Sunday morning began like any typical
Sunday with two boys under the age of four.
Susan and I have always been consistent early risers.
Having two boys up at the crack of dawn and running
all day until bedtime sustained our early morning
discipline. As a military family we also prided
ourselves in the structure, order, and efficiency of
home management. Susan was even then, as she does
today, teaching workshops to professional women's
groups on "How to Make Household Management
Manageable." We were the model of efficiency – but
not this Sunday.

A few weeks before this fateful Sunday, I had been offered and accepted the invitation to serve as the interim pianist for our church worship service. I had always enjoyed playing for my own personal enjoyment but had never performed in recitals or even played for family gatherings. Needless to say I was a bit anxious and starting to have second thoughts about my ability and my willingness to be in a position to not "be at my best." So on this particular Sunday morning I was very focused on our getting ready on time and arriving at the church early enough for me to cram in some extra rehearsal time.

The boys were up and running as Susan and I worked through our shared routine of breakfast, baths, and dressing. Diaper bags were inspected and lined up on the counter along with Bibles and most importantly the music for the worship service. We were on schedule and all systems "go" as they say at NASA. We were on time for our departure; me grabbing the bags and boys, Susan retrieving the Bibles, and as I assumed my all-important music. In good military order we were off to enjoy a wonderful morning of worship and fellowship.

As we pulled into the church parking lot, I told Susan that I would get the boys settled in their respective classes if she would go ahead and take my music into the sanctuary area. It was at this point she informed me that she did not have my music. "WHAT?" In an unbelievable near incredulous tone I said, "It was sitting right next to the Bibles. How could you not pick it up and bring it when you got the Bibles?" Of course I did not communicate this to her when we were leaving the house. I naturally *assumed* that since I had the boys she would pick up the music when she got the Bibles.

So here we are at church, with me already in a heightened level of anxiety only to discover I have to take another thirty minutes to race home and race back to church and . . . well by this time I think you have the mental picture. I began to unload my anxiety on my wife. Angry and yelling, demeaning and condescending words spewed from my mouth as I barked orders to my wife about taking the younger son, I would keep our older son, hurry and get out of the car, and how could you be so stupid as to not pick up the music.

Speeding home I am justifying my behavior and finding every way I can for not having to accept any responsibility for what just happened. We were leading and teaching a marriage enrichment group at this time with the focus of developing Christ like behavior in the husband. I was convinced that what we were teaching was exactly what couples really needed to take their marriages to the next spiritual level. In my heart I knew I was resenting the level of responsibility the Bible places on the husband being the spiritual leader of his home. Now I was taking this opportunity to vent my resentment, and I was wrong.

As if hearing from the Lord in my heart was not enough conviction, I glanced in the rear view mirror to see my little son with a sad countenance and a look of fear. "Michael," I said, "Everything is all right. Daddy should not have yelled at mommy. I lost my temper and it was not mommy's fault. I am sorry. Will you forgive me for yelling at mommy?" Now as only a little toddler can do, he immediately began to smile and said, "That's okay daddy, I forgive you. And don't feel bad, I will help you find your temper."

Now we have enjoyed the laughter of retelling this story over the years having forgotten the pain of the moment in my precious little son's willingness to help me "find my temper." Unfortunately, we never had to search far to find that temper for any time I felt inconvenienced or interrupted or when things did not go just like military precision, my anger always seemed capable of finding its way home without anyone having to go look for it. What I did not know then was my response was a reactive response based on my own sense of lofty, unfulfilled, and unrealistic expectations of my wife and children. What is even more ironic is that I was teaching Sunday school classes, home Bible studies, and leading marriage enrichment small groups and just could not seem to be able to practice at home with any degree of consistency what I was teaching to others. It is amazing how under times of stress and fatigue, or when someone is pushing our buttons as we say, the times when we really need to act the most like Jesus, we tend to react and behave more like the devil. What I did not know then about taking personal responsibility for my actions was a lot. What I did not know then about triggering events and reactive or inactive responses to life events and my power to actually choose my response was a lot. Even with a heart's desire to walk in the fruit of the Spirit, I continually found myself meandering in the works of the flesh. If you have ever felt that frustration or are still floundering around in your spiritual growing process then read on.

This book is the result of over thirty years of marriage, family, and work relationships trying to crack the code on doing what I teach. The fundamental ideas and the tools that will be presented to you provide the answer to not only *knowing what to do* to live a life that models the character and nature of Jesus but *how to change your behavior* so you actually live your life being transformed into the image of the Son of God. We are going to close the gap between knowing what to do and actually begin behaving in a way that demonstrates we have died to the life of sin and the flesh and entered into a newness of life in the Son of God. This is a life lived in the Spirit creating a harvest in the fruit of the Spirit (Gal. 5:22). Every significant *breakthrough* in life begins with a *break with* something else – *we must die to one life before we can enter another.*

In the pages that follow I am going to ask you to make a commitment to a life long journey of learning. I am going to introduce to you a model for personal transformation based on the concept of personal mastery. Personal mastery is a growth process, a maturation process that is evidenced and clearly used by the apostle Paul in all of his New Testament writings. A master craftsman, like a Michelangelo, becomes passionate and committed to a lifelong learning of a calling. In this sense mastery becomes a process of maturing through four distinct and integrated stages of development and an unwavering commitment to excellence. Understanding these four stages and learning to apply a few vital habits will create the foundation for living an abundant life in Jesus Christ. Master these and you transform into the nature and image of the Son of God.

You will see that I am going to be intentionally repetitive, writing many times throughout these pages that your life is the sum product of your choices. You are facing one of those choices now. Your choice is clear. Stay where you are and continue to struggle or begin a new journey of personal transformation as you discover that "I can do all things through Christ who strengthens me" (Phil, 4:13). Stop wasting today wishing for a better yesterday and start creating the reality for a better tomorrow. As you prepare to read on, ponder this – you say you believe in God and His Son Jesus Christ – so when are you going to start acting like it?

Defining the Abundant Life in Christ

Being saved does not automatically guarantee nor give people the ability to live fruitful, effective, and abundant Christian lives. The apostle Paul writes in his letter to the Ephesians this exhortation:

> *"I, therefore, a prisoner for the Lord, beg you to lead a life worthy of the calling to which you have been called."* (Ephesians 4.1)

Paul also wrote that there is power in this walk with the Spirit to not fulfill the lusts of the flesh (Gal 5:16). He then goes on to describe the fruit of the

Spirit, what is supposed to be evident in the conduct of authentic Christian behavior. In the midst of the blessing of physical prosperity in America, we can easily be misled to believe that the abundant life in Christ is about material prosperity, material abundance. A careful and complete reading of the Bible will show you that the fruit of the Spirit, lived in the biblical concept, is at the heart of living an abundant life in Christ. Abundant life in Christ is not about what you have. It is about who you are and what you do and the contentment to know that even living in abject physical poverty "the joy of the Lord is my strength."

Our walk in the Spirit is something we are compelled to do by the apostle Paul. The authentic Christian lives in the Spirit walking with the Spirit and lives a life free from sin in the power of the Holy Spirit. Living a transformed and abundant life in Christ is more than being saved and making mental assent to biblical doctrine. Being transformed and living in spiritual abundance requires that we seek after God and the things above. That we put off the old man in the flesh, and we put on the new man who is renewed (transformed) in knowledge after the image of Jesus Christ (Col. 3:1-15).

The apostle Paul literally begs us to live a life worthy of God's calling. He pleads with us in several of his letters to die to the ways of the world, live in holiness, engage in spiritual transformation, to renew our minds, to buffet our flesh, and to run the race to win the crown of glory (Ephesians 4:17-20; Romans 8:12-13; Galatians 5:16-17; I Peter 1:14-16;

Romans 12:1-2; Ephesians 4:22-24; Matthew 11:28-30). When other people look at you, can they see the changes in your character and your behavior? People who knew you before you made your profession of faith and who know you now, can they tell that you are different? Can you tell that you are different in your thoughts, desires, attitudes, goals, and key motivational drivers for your life? Are you growing in your spiritual development, or have you been side lined in your spiritual walk?

How we choose to answer these questions is reflective of how well we understand the need to cultivate spiritual disciplines in our lives. The first discipline that is absolutely essential to your spiritual growth is daily Bible reading. Everything we need to learn about God, salvation, reconciliation, holiness, our spiritual growth, and our spiritual walk – all the essentials of an authentic and abundant life in Christ, we learn from the Bible. This is why the first discipline we need to cultivate as we are transformed into the image and character of Jesus Christ is daily reading and studying the Word of God. If you fall in love with reading the Bible, you will discover the keys to living in the Spirit, and your life will demonstrate the fruit of the Spirit in your thinking, your attitude, your emotions, and your behavior. Walk in the Spirit and you shall not fulfill the lusts of the flesh.

The apostle Peter wrote in his second epistle that unless we cultivate and make daily spiritual disciplines a part of our lives, we will live "ineffective and unfruitful in the knowledge of our Lord Jesus Christ." As a result, every authentic Christian has an obligation to learn and to practice these fundamental disciplines to live the abundant life that Jesus came to offer us all. The process of spiritual transformation is not a work of the flesh but a work produced by the power of the Holy Spirit. We can quench this power, and we can try to make ourselves over in our own image rather than the image and character of Jesus Christ.

A life of spiritual transformation is not a self-help course or some extreme makeover according to the principles and practices of worldly philosophy (Col 2:8). God has provided the means for us to be transformed into the image of His Son. The key is what are we doing with this knowledge and power He has provided to us? Well Titus tells us what we are to do. "For the grace of God that brings salvation has appeared to all men, teaching us that denying ungodliness and worldly lusts, we should live soberly, righteously, and godly in this present world" (Titus 2:11-12). To live soberly means to manage our lives well. By cooperating with the power of the Holy Spirit, an authentic Christian is to be Spirit-disciplined and Spirit-controlled not just self-disciplined and self-controlled.

Authentic Christians who are living the abundant life in Christ are deeply committed to and sold out to living under the authority and the power of the Holy Spirit. As such, they are deeply committed to pursuing excellence in Jesus and demonstrating His character, His nature, and His conduct and behavior in every aspect of their lives. Every day these authentic Christians are seeking to continually learn and grow in the development of their spiritual walk. Christ rules in their hearts, and He is their treasure. All their dreams, hopes, aspirations, passion, and ambitions are surrendered over to God's will and sovereignty for their lives.

Authentic Christians who choose to live "soberly, righteously, and godly" have tremendous awareness of their strengths and weaknesses recognizing how their habits and behavior affect the lives of both fellow believers and non-believers alike. They are fully aware that any lapse into sin brings reproach and shame on the name of the Lord Jesus Christ. Consequently, authentic Christians take responsibility and accountability for their thinking, attitude, and behavior. They never blame shift, make excuses, nor become a victim of life's circumstances. They live in abundance in their core beliefs, are creative in problem solving, are committed to excellence in Christ, and like the apostle Paul, they can sing songs of praise in the middle of life's most difficult circumstances, trials, and struggles.

Like the apostle Paul, authentic Christians know they are on a mission from God and stay "on message." They are guided by a compass not a map, and are flexible, agile, trusting God completely to align His goals and purposes for their lives to fulfill the ministry to which He has called them. Taking heed to Paul's words (Romans 12), they are renewing their minds daily to keep their thoughts aligned with the core principles of the Bible, seeking to develop the mind of Christ and be proactive in their thinking and not reactive to events and circumstances that challenge their walk in the Spirit. Consequently, authentic Christians keep a kingdom focus and keep growing and transforming into the nature and character of their Lord and Savior Jesus Christ.

Are you ready for the challenge of change? Are you ready to lay aside the pretense of calling yourself a Christian in name only? If so, read on my friend and discover the power of metamorphosis. There is an authentic life in Christ waiting for you. Let go of the old lie that people cannot change. Any person can change who has the desire to do so. There is an abundant life in Christ waiting for you. All you have to do is reach out and receive it. Salvation is not the end of the journey for authentic Christians but the beginning of a journey to spiritual transformation and spiritual abundance in the fruit of the Spirit. So keep reading and enjoy the discovery of the life in Christ that is waiting for you.

Part One

A Better Way of Coming Down the Stairs

Chapter One

Why We Resist Change

God grant me the serenity to accept the people I cannot change, the courage to change the one I can, and the wisdom to know it's me.
~Author Unknown

A fundamental concept for a Christian to remember is that our life in Christ is going to be full of changes and a part of us just does not want to do it. That part of you that is resisting being changed the Bible calls your flesh. Fortunately, we have the Holy Spirit to help us change once we make our profession of faith. Unfortunately, there is so much confusion over the purpose of the Holy Spirit in the life of a believer that most people are left to fend for themselves and that explains why so many Christians struggle in their transformation process. Absent of the proper understanding of the Holy Spirit in your life, you are left to try and control and will yourself into a spiritual transformation using your flesh as the primary tool. Guess what? You cannot use your flesh to do what your flesh is continually resisting – transformation. Even neuroscience has now begun to discover that there are physical parts of the brain that resist change. I will be discussing later about how our brain physically works against our conscience effort and desire to change our habits. For now, trust me that your brain takes a path of least resistance until it encounters some overwhelming and compelling need to change. So even science proves it – your flesh is not your friend, your guide, your counselor, or your teacher when it comes to change and transformation. Your flesh will do anything it can to keep you from transforming into the nature and character of Jesus. So don't trust your flesh to help you change – you have to command and discipline your flesh as you take personal responsibility for your behavior and discover the purpose of the Holy Spirit in your life to lead you in your transformation process.

Not only do we have the Holy Spirit to help us in this matter of putting our flesh to death and lead us into spiritual maturity, the church is also supposed to be playing a role and serving that function as well. The Bible tells us that the fundamental responsibility of a church is to equip the saints (Eph. 4:11-12). Equipping carries with it a connotation of preparing an army for battle. From my military days I know that it takes nearly three times as many support personnel behind the lines to support one war fighter on the front line of the battlefield. Equipping is hard work, and the church, in its equipping role, must do this work to develop and organize itself as a learning organization to fulfill its role in the life of the believer. Learning organizations are themselves grounded on fundamental disciplines of behavior and must preach, teach, practice, and master these disciplines in the individual lives of their members. Jesus was many things, but woven into the fabric of his daily behavior was his teaching role with his disciples. Similarly, Paul was the consummate teacher of the gospel. Note that in the letter to the Ephesians, the apostle Paul exhorts his disciples to *measure up* to the fullness of Christ and to *grow up* in all things into Christ (Eph. 4:13-16). Here we see the beauty of this relationship – the Church is to equip and the saints are to grow up to fulfill the purpose of being built up in Christ to accomplish the work He has for us to do. You are saved and disciplined for a purpose – the hope and glory of Christ in you. *Is that not just unbelievable!*

As an educator, coach, life skills facilitator, corporate learning professional, and pastor, I was haunted for the solution to an age old problem, namely, why when given the opportunity to learn, the need to learn, the crisis of life that compels someone to learn something new to achieve a different result, people choose not to change? Another way of asking this question is, "Why don't we grow up?" Have you ever shared this same frustration? If you are a parent I know you have felt this burden with your children. You teach, you plead, you beg, you scold, you admonish, you exhort, you bribe, you yell, and in the final agony of despair you cry out, "when are they ever going to *learn? When are they ever going to get it?"*

Change is a dynamic that knows no organizational, geographic, ethnic, gender, or world-view boundaries. As human beings we all have the same fundamental, emotional, mental and physical reactions, and responses to change – we don't like it, and we resist it. Even change we desire we still find ourselves fighting, resisting, lapsing back to comfortable, reactive or at best inactive responses to change we know will not take us closer to achieving our legitimate needs, wants, goals, and desires. Organizational expert Peter Senge may have said it best when he wrote,"people don't resist change. They resist being changed!"

By change I am talking about the fundamental aspect of *becoming* different and *behaving* in a different way – of passing from one state of existence to another. I place these two words *becoming* and *behaving* in this specific order for, as you will read later, what we *do* is a fundamental byproduct of who we *are*; hence, what we are *becoming* leads to how we will *behave*. The word that best describes this kind of change is *metamorphosis,* derived from both Latin and Greek meaning to *transform*. A great example to guide us in the use of this word is a monarch butterfly that goes through a metamorphosis, a transformation, of four distinct developmental stages of life. Likewise, we who call ourselves Christians also pass through what I believe to be four distinct stages of maturity in our growth in Jesus Christ. In the development of the monarch butterfly if there is a disruption of any of these four life cycle stages, then we do not see the beauty of the final and total transformation process of the butterfly. So too, if you do not pass through and experience the interdependence of the four distinct stages of growth in Christ, you too do not exhibit your beauty nor get to live your life in the total transformation of your spiritual growth and development.

I meet people every day struggling in some very difficult life events. Working in healthcare, I see patient, their families, and hospital staff, in physical, emotional, and spiritual distress every day. Recently I spoke with a mom whose little six-year-old daughter had just completed her tenth surgical spine procedure and was facing at least ten more surgeries. She had nearly died twice already as a result of her medical condition. This mom was wiped out. During three hours of intense conversation with me, I was able to lead her through some fundamental beliefs, helping her to change her focus, and giving her the strength and encouragement from God's Word to see more clearly about how to choose her responses and frame her attitude in this life event.

What about you? Are you living your life abundantly or just trying to survive through another day? Have you read other books about being positive, self-help books that read like cotton candy – great to the taste but fizzle without any permanent change taking place in your beliefs, thoughts, emotions, and behavior? What if I could show you a way to cut through all the other fad programs, behavior modification techniques, hocus pocus change your focus, magic wands and pixie dust, and Oprah's book of the month approaches to achieving real breakthrough behavior change to compel you into an abundant walk in the Spirit? Would you try one more time?

LEARNING TO CHANGE

The poet Yeats quipped that, "Learning is not about filling a pail but the lighting of a fire." At the end of one semester while teaching at the United States Military Academy at West Point, a cadet summarized his learning experience with me in the classroom. He wrote that our time together was well spent, and he appreciated my enthusiasm and passion as a teacher, and then followed the proverbial "but." He went on to create an analogy that my task as his professor was like Hercules cleaning the manure out the Augean stables. Now that is quite a feat considering how many horses were in those stables. So the cadet wrote that while I had accomplished the Herculean task of cleaning all the manure out of his mind, for which he was grateful, he was left wanting in that I had not filled the void that was left behind. I too felt a loss at his predicament though I never believed it my place to fill the mind of any student but instead ignite a flame and create the passion and desire of filling it for themselves with the pathway and process by which one seeks for and finds truth, meaning, value, and purpose in life.

The apostle Paul exemplifies for me the quintessential teacher in that he demonstrates not only the ability to impart truth, wisdom, and knowledge, the filling of the bucket, but he also inspires his reader to engage these virtues in conduct and behavior that produces the fire to pursue excellence in living an abundant life in Christ. Note the emphasis here is that we are supposed to be standing in, walking in, and living in, the abundant life in Jesus Christ. Paul preached the gospel to bring people to the truth and reality of Jesus Christ; he then taught people the gospel so they could grow up and mature in the nature and character of Christ. The apostle James in his letter echoes Paul as he exhorted his "students" to not be mere hearers of the gospel (James 1:2). He goes on to reprove them for the failure to change their behavior having heard the truth of God's Word. In the midst of this systematic approach to what is supposed to be a transformation from a life lived in the flesh satisfying selfish gain and ambitious, fleshly, lustful desires to a life lived in the Spirit, Paul unashamedly scolded and rebuked so-called believers over the entire Asian continent for not walking in the light of the truth to which they were called and had received from his teaching (Col. 3:12-17).

The Pauline Model of Behavior Change

Within the text of the New Testament we see what I call the Pauline Model for behavior change: Preaching – Teaching – Exhorting – Reproving.

We preach the gospel to bring people to Jesus Christ. We teach the gospel to grow people in the nature of Jesus Christ. We exhort people to get them to live in behavior that models Jesus Christ. We reprove people to hold then accountable for failing to conform to the character of Christ.

As the monarch caterpillar moves from stage to stage in developmental transformation, so too the young believer is *supposed* to progress through the process of spiritual development that translates into daily practical behavior. How silly would it look to see the transformed monarch butterfly crawling around in the dirt rather than taking to flight? How tragic it is to see Christians who should be soaring in their relationship with Jesus Christ barely able to stand, holding on to objects to brace themselves, timid in the understanding of their freedom to fly as they clutch to the corrupting things of this world.

Where the Church Is Failing

It should be very clear, at this point, that the Church has been negligent in understanding and teaching the dynamics and disciplines of a learning organization. By *the Church*, I mean the body of local believers, who congregate together for the purpose of fellowship, prayer, the equipping of the saints and breaking of bread, and its requisite leaders (Acts 2:42-47). Sadly, many churches, I do not mean to indict all churches, have become a "feel good – baby boomer-country club-behavior tolerant-respectable membership" defined by the sociological "do good" projects and psychological "feel good" philosophy that the apostle Paul spoke against and sternly rebuked in virtually every one of his New Testament letters.

If the Church is to regain relevance in the lives of so-called authentic Christians, to regain relevance in the moral and social fabric of cultures, not just the American culture but a prevailing and sustaining world view, then church leadership must return *the Church* to her roots of Biblical preaching, teaching, exhorting, and reproving. People cannot become what their churches and church leaders are not.

Life Long Commitment to Learning

The apostle Paul pleaded with the new believers of the first century church to be disciplined and committed to a life long process of physical, emotional, and spiritual transformation. He expected his effort in teaching them the gospel to have power to transform their lives. Paul created what world-renowned leadership and learning experts today call a "sustained impact-learning program." These experts in leadership and learning development have created learning models that transcend just conveying information and transferring knowledge data. Intellectual intelligence is great for learning simple addition or the Pythagorean Theorem. Unfortunately, learning to change behavior requires something more than intellectual intelligence. Change requires self-awareness and empathy and a host of other skills related to what has become known as emotional intelligence.

Any of you who have experienced a formal learning model, you have been exposed to something akin to the following. You sit in an instructor led environment, like the typical classroom with a teacher who has knowledge about a particular subject. The teacher gives you, the student, knowledge in a form of a lecture coupled with a video presentation, graphics, computer simulation, and Internet connected topical sites. The intent is that students use all this acquired knowledge to make choices about their behavior in a host of related or unrelated activities. Sounds like a lot of churches today with their high tech video and slide show sermonettes.

What we have discovered along the way of studying the effects of this model is that making choices is more than you knowing the data, understanding the data, and having the data right. Ideas have power to influence thinking, and thinking drives attitudes that ultimately compel behavior. Behavior change, as it turns out, is not just acquiring knowledge and understanding effective thinking. It also requires a coupling together various emotions that bring the compelling drive for change. Note the primary objective of teaching something is to impact thinking with an ultimate goal of influencing behavior somewhere along the line or within the learning system. Surprisingly for those of us who teach professionally, behavior change takes place much more through an emotional-driven process with people creating word pictures and mental models "seeing" as it were in their mind's eye. This experience that neuroscience and learning industry experts are calling "emotional experiential memory", EEM, creates the force of momentum that in turn changes behavior. Real learning makes an emotional connection with you, and unless you feel the consequences of not changing to more effective habits and behaviors, you stay in the rut of your comfort habits that will not lead to your abundant life in Christ.

Real change in your life must satisfy two fundamental questions to override the physiology of your brain to sustain the status quo. First you must be convicted of your need to change. This means you recognize that change is going to be beneficial to you. Second, you must be convinced that you are capable of change. If you do not believe you are capable of changing, you will not change. If you lack the desire or will to change, then you will not change either. You may become a believer in Jesus Christ. You may ask and receive forgiveness of your sins. Until you believe choosing not to sin is in your best interest, you will continue to cycle in the rut of sin and forgiveness and live in defeat and frustration as a casualty of spiritual warfare. The Bible provides us the answer about whether we can change. The Bible tells us that we have the ability, the capacity to change. What God, the Bible, and no one else can do for you is make those choices for you. Only you can do that for yourself. Only you can say yes to the "want to" and the "can do" for personal transformation in your life. So time to ask yourself again, do you want to change? Do you believe you can change? Do you want to live free from the cycle of sin and guilt and pain and scars of disobedience? Here is a little story from the Internet of unknown origin that might help you with your answers.

SCARS OF LIFE

Some years ago, on a hot summer day in South Florida, a little boy decided to go for a swim in the old swimming hole behind his house. In a hurry to dive into the cool water, he ran out the back door, leaving behind shoes, socks, and shirt as he went.

He flew into the water, not realizing that as he swam toward the middle of the lake, an alligator was swimming toward the shore. His father, working in the yard, saw the two as they got closer and closer together. In utter fear, he ran toward the water, yelling to his son as loudly as he could.

Hearing his voice, the little boy became alarmed and made a U-turn to swim to his father. It was too late. Just as he reached his father, the alligator reached him. From the dock, the father grabbed his little boy by the arms just as the alligator snatched his legs.

That began an incredible tug-of-war between the two. The alligator was much stronger than the father, but the father was much too passionate to let go. A farmer happened to drive by, heard his screams, raced from his truck with a rifle, took aim and shot the alligator.

Remarkably, after weeks and weeks in the hospital, the little boy survived. His legs were extremely scarred by the vicious attack of the animal. And, on his arms, were deep scratches where his father's fingernails dug into his flesh in his effort to hang on to the son he loved.

The newspaper reporter, who interviewed the boy after the trauma of the event had passed, asked if he would show him his scars. The boy lifted his pant legs. And then, with obvious pride, he said to the reporter, 'But look at my arms. I have great scars on my arms, too. I have them because my Dad wouldn't let go.'

You and I can identify with that little boy. We have scars too but not from an alligator. They are the scars of a painful past. Some of those scars are unsightly and have caused us deep regret. But, some wounds, my friend, are because God has refused to let go. In the midst of your struggle, He's been there holding on to you.

The Scripture teaches that God loves you. You are a child of God. He wants to protect you and provide for you in every way. But sometimes we foolishly wade into dangerous situations, not knowing what lies ahead. The swimming hole of life is filled with peril and we forget that the enemy is waiting to attack. That's when the tug-of-war begins - and if you have the scars of His love on your arms, be very, very grateful. He did not and will not ever let you go.

Do you want to change? Do you believe you can change? Do you want to live free from the cycle of sin and guilt and pain and the scars of disobedience? Then read on my friend, read on.

Chapter Two

God's Plan And Process For Change

)

Everyone thinks of changing the world, but no one thinks of changing himself. ~ Leo Tolstoy

Since you have made it this far in the book, it is likely safe for me to assume that you are committed to learning the key life skills needed to embrace change and grow in your spiritual walk. In the following chapters you will see that God has provided us with the means to cooperate with the Holy Spirit in our transformation process. You must understand that God does not compel us to change. He provides us the means and invites and encourages us to change. Understand too that you can choose not to change. Lacking the desire to change, you can choose to live in spiritual poverty. It makes no rational sense to make that choice. Unfortunately, I meet people everyday making that very choice and then wondering why they lack the joy of the Spirit.

Oswald Chambers, writing in his devotional, *My Utmost for His Highest,* stated the following:

> We cannot do what God does and God will not do what we can do. We cannot save ourselves nor sanctify ourselves, God does that; but God will not give us good habits, He will not give us character, He will not make us walk aright. We have to do all that for ourselves, we have to work out the salvation that God has worked in.

God continues to allow us to exercise our free will in cooperating with Him in the spiritual transformation of our lives. If this were not so, then much of what the apostle Paul wrote regarding how we *once* lived, our former lives, and what we can *be* in our resurrected life in Christ makes no logical sense. Paul tells us that we have resurrection power in Jesus Christ (Phil. 3:10). I love the Greek word for power, *dunamis* that gives us our English word for dynamite. There is a difference, however, in having power and releasing that power in your life. A vacuum cleaner has all kinds of potential and stored power to suck up dirt. Unless you plug it in and turn it on, you are just wasting your time pushing it back and forth over a piece of soiled carpet. The resurrection power of Jesus has disarmed and triumphed over all principalities and powers (Col. 2:15). That means none of your past or current habits that are limiting your growth and maturity in your walk in the Spirit have control over you. None of your emotions have control over you, and your thinking does not have control over you. Your past life and the choices of your past also have no control over you. The good news of this biblical truth means you can change if you want to change. We have the personal responsibility to cooperate with God and do our part in our spiritual transformation process. This story will help us see the real problem.

A young man left his native Ireland to try to make a new life and fresh start in America. His aging mother was unwilling to leave her beloved country even in the midst of some very difficult daily circumstances of the culture at the time. Her young son promised he would send her financial support once he was able to establish himself in the hope of the American dream.

With hard work and good fortune, the young man established and grew his own business into a thriving and expanding industry. He would send newspaper articles home to his mother urging her to come to America and enjoy the blessings of his transformed life. She continued to refuse his offers to join him in his blessing to her. Extremely proud of her son's accomplishments, she was eager to share the news of his good fortune with all her neighbors. Unfortunately, her neighbors did not take so kindly to knowing about the blessings of her son while she continued to live in abject poverty. How could he have failed to provide for her in the midst of his abundant blessings?

One day the mother discovered the scorn of her neighbors in a conversation about her son's continued prosperity. "Why does he not help you? Why has he not sent you anything to help you in your circumstances?" they asked. The mother replied that her son had sent her pretty pictures with every one of his letters. Eager to show her neighbors, she invited them into her little cottage, opened a chest, and proceeded to show them stacks of pictures of Benjamin Franklin on one hundred dollar bills. All this time she was in possession of tremendous wealth and continued to live in abject poverty not understanding the value of her "pretty pictures."

I wonder how often we too are unaware of the resources provided to us by our heavenly Father as we mistake them for "pretty pictures." This young man was providing his mother with the power and the means to move beyond her present circumstances. Lacking understanding, she was unable to exercise and appropriate that power to change herself and her circumstances. God and the monarch butterfly work in a wonderful partnership in the physical changes and transformation from one stage of life to another. We too must partner with God through the knowledge of His Word and the leading of the Holy Spirit for our spiritual transformation as well.

In summation, human beings have the capacity and the ability to change. Whenever I hear someone say, "I can't help myself," I kindly but assertively remind them – oh yes you can! As other change experts have written before me, between any stimuli and our response to those stimuli we have the capacity to stop, think, and choose our response. We can choose to be different; we can choose to change our thinking and our habits. Some of these changes may be very hard, but they are not impossible. Your thinking and your habits are things you have acquired and are not born into you. Since they are not innate then you have the ability to change even though you may lack the will and desire to change. Let me say again, no one is going to force you to change, but unless you are willing to believe you can change and choose to do so, you will never walk in the full assurance and abundance of spiritual blessings that God desires to give to you. The choice is yours.

Behavior Change From Behavioral Learning

Throughout his New Testament writings, whether he was aware of it by training or inspiration of the Holy Spirit, teaching the gospel and exhorting behavior change by integrating aspects of EEM and mental models is something the apostle Paul did on a consistent basis. As such, I never cease to be amazed when Biblical truth is discovered by those wise in the ways of the world and then used to explain life in the physical world in which we live.

One of Paul's most powerful uses of EEM to create a compelling experience and stimulate an emotional connection to learning was the use of a form of Roman punishment to convey a spiritual principle. In various New Testament passages, Paul writes about sin and sin nature as a corrupt, decaying, dead, human body (Romans 5:5-14). Paul is demonstrating for his disciples the literal form of punishment where a prisoner would be physically chained to the dead body of another prisoner. You also get an immediate emotional reaction, do you not, with the thought of being chained to a dead body? Can you imagine the smell, the flies, and the wild dogs lurking about in anticipation of eating this rotting corpse? Quite an emotional picture to say the least, is it not? So knowing that sin in you (a person who, according to Romans 5:6-11, has *supposedly* made a profession of faith, to be dead to sin and alive to Christ), can contaminate, infect, and destroy your life, why would you persist in making yourself a slave to sin and its ultimate death? It is completely illogical and irrational for you to do things that you know are going to bring pain into your life.

When you understand the power in the process of creating compelling, emotional, mental images –EEM - you can use this tool to intentionally create compelling narratives and memory experiences. In doing so, you can use the emotional impact they create to change your behavior. Your flesh, the world, and the devil are not your friends. In an unholy alliance they work together to keep you chained to corruption and death disguised as the fun and entertainment of the life you once lived. Paul tells us to take off that old life and discard it like filthy rags and to put on the holy garments of righteousness and walk in freedom from the lusts of this world.

Self-Control versus EEM

Many of us no doubt grew up with difficult circumstances in our lives from time to time. We all can remember a well-meaning parent or teacher's attempt to encourage us in these times with words like, "suck it up," or "pull yourself together," or "what doesn't kill you makes you stronger." These admonishers may have meant well but self-control, while serving some limited use as a life skill, is not sufficient for creating or sustaining long term results in beliefs, thoughts, attitudes, and behaviors. No doubt you have experienced your own now long forgotten resolutions that wilted under the pressure of stress, fatigue, or sheer unwillingness to give up what you knew to be self-defeating and self-sabotaging thinking and behavior.

When the apostle Paul encourages believers to "walk in the Spirit," he is suggesting a lot more than merely making resolutions and demanding that we pull ourselves up by our bootstraps. Paul is indicating that there are key practical behaviors we are to engage in that allow us to cooperate with the power of the Holy Spirit that will drive impacting and life sustaining change in our beliefs, thoughts, attitudes, and actions. Paul tells us that in Christ we have a new character (Col 3: 12-17). He tells us specifically that we are to take off our old nature, literally in the original language to strip it off, like taking off a filthy set of clothes. We are then to redress, to put on those behaviors that are of the nature and character of Christ. This requires active effort on *our* part. This requires great purpose and intentional behavior on *our* part. We are to take off the old and put on the new in Christ. EEM is self-regulation where we create experiential memory to inform us of past experiences that propel us to wiser and more effective choices in the present. Paul does this continually throughout his writings where he reminds us of the pain of walking in darkness, our former self (Col 3:1-11). How what we did in our past caused us great pain and separation from God. Then he tells us that since we *are in* Christ, what the new self is to look like, sound like, think like, and act like. This is the functional element of creating emotional experiential memory. So now, once we do our part, the Holy Spirit can take over and do His part in the miracle metamorphosis of your life.

What I am advocating here is neither a works oriented salvation nor worldly, psychological techniques. You really have to be careful not to dismiss what I am saying through a previously established thinking bias. Let me spell it out for you as clearly as I can. We are saved by grace through faith in the finished work of the death and resurrection of Jesus Christ. What I am advocating is that once we are saved, submitting to the Lordship of Jesus Christ and pursuing to live in the Spirit and walk in the Spirit, requires our commitment and dedication – our effort to pursue excellence in right living. Failing to understand this fundamental biblical truth, you are left to regress into your old thinking and your old habits and miss out on the abundant life in Christ lived in obedience and passion to the Word of God. You even risk the possibility of falling away from God's grace. We are to continue in God's goodness (Romans 11:22) or risk being cut off. Paul wrote in 1 Thessalonians 4:1-8:

> Furthermore then we beseech you, brethren, and exhort you by the Lord Jesus, that as ye have received of us how ye ought to walk and to please God, so ye would abound more and more. For ye know what commandments we gave you by the Lord Jesus. For this is the will of God, even your sanctification . . . .

The exhortation and encouragement of this passage is that God calls us to a holy life. This holy life requires us to yield to the power of the Holy Spirit, dwelling within us, to control all innate fleshly desires and impulses. This is not self-control but spirit-control of my flesh. I have to release this power, tap into this power and through obedience to the teaching of the gospel, and avoid quenching this power in my life. It also shows Paul's concern for the practical principles we are to live out in our lives cooperating with the Holy Spirit in leading, guiding, and bringing to our minds all that Jesus taught regarding a holy life.

A Response to Skeptics and Cynics

Why should you keep reading this book? That is a fair question and one I always ask myself while browsing through a bookstore or reading an electronic advertisement in my email. The answer is simple – you need to learn how to take responsibility for change and the transformation process of growing up in Jesus Christ. This book offers you that opportunity. We live in a world today that is constantly bombarding us with messages about what we need to be happy, joyful, and content. We are flooded with opportunity after opportunity for grabbing all the gusto and living the lifestyle of the rich and famous. Even within the Church, we are being tempted and teased to accept what Paul warned as "another gospel than that which I preached to you" (Gal. 1:6-9). The brutal reality is that we live in a world of tremendous uncertainty, change at an ever increasing rate, and the ambivalence of fluctuating and diametrically opposed emotions. So let me ask you in the brutal reality of the world in which you live – how are your habits working for you? Going again to the writing of Paul in 2 Thessalonians 3:4-7:

> We are confident of you in the Lord that what we instruct you, you are doing and will continue to do. May the Lord direct your hearts to the love of God and to the endurance of Christ. We instruct you, brothers, in the name of (our) Lord Jesus Christ, to shun any brother who conducts himself in a disorderly way and not according to the tradition they received from us. For you know how one must imitate us.

Notice the method, the mechanics of behavior, illustrated by the apostle Paul to these new believers: 1) receive instruction, 2) do and continue to do what you were instructed, 3) yield to God for Him to change your heart, 4) avoid those who will not conform so they do not mislead you, and 5) copy and imitate our example of how we behave in the Lord.

Within the church I pastor and in my daily work with people in the professional setting, I have discovered fundamental patterns of human behavior that require a different level of learning. If we are going to truly change, transform if you will, in the biblical sense, we must rise above the cares of this life to live in the joy and the contentment of the Spirit the Bible promises. In essence, I give you this challenge. If you say you are a Bible-believing-Born Again-water baptized- Spirit filled-evangelical Christian – who I will refer to as an authentic Christian - why are you not *acting* like it? In other words, why are the choices, behaviors, attitudes, emotions, and thinking in your life not reflective of what you say you believed?

The Answer

I have waited a long time to write this book, in part, because I was not sure I had anything new and original to add to the already exhaustive list of books on personal life transformation, change, peak performance, and living your best life now, as they say. Then one day during a break in one of my seminars for continuing medical education, one of the students approached me and said that what I was teaching about personal transformation, change, accountability, and managing personal responses to life's events was really hitting home with her. She wanted to know if she could have a copy of my book.

I regretted having to tell her at the time that I did not have a book published. When she proceeded to ask me why, I somewhat jokingly stated that I did not think anyone would read it. She looked at me with a kind smile and simply said, "I would."

How wonderful it is to have someone believe in us. I want you to know that I believe in you and so does your heavenly Father. History is full of life's failures and God's reclamation projects. Need I remind you of Abraham who had a problem with telling the truth? Then there was Moses who had this problem with his temper and murder, Isaac and his self-will, and Jacob with his deceit. Dare we not forget Samson and his fleshly lusts along with David and his betrayal of his mighty men of valor during his sin with Bathsheba? Consider if you will, the life of one of history's greatest failures who persisted to the highest level of personal and moral achievement.

YEAR	FAILURES or SETBACKS	SUCCESSES
1832	Lost job Defeated for state legislature	Elected company captain of Illinois militia in Black Hawk War
1833	Failed in business	Appointed postmaster of New Salem, Illinois Appointed deputy surveyor of Sangamon County

1834		Elected to Illinois state legislature
1835	**Sweetheart died**	
1836	**Had nervous breakdown**	Re-elected to Illinois state legislature (running first in his district) Received license to practice law in Illinois state courts
1837		Led Whig delegation in moving Illinois state capital from Vandalia to Springfield Became law partner of John T. Stuart
1838	**Defeated for Speaker**	Nominated for Illinois House Speaker by Whig caucus Re-elected to Illinois House (running first in his district) Served as Whig floor leader
1839		Chosen presidential elector by first Whig convention Admitted to practice law in U.S. Circuit Court

1840		Argues first case before Illinois Supreme Court Re-elected to Illinois state legislature
1841		Established new law practice with Stephen T. Logan
1842		Admitted to practice law in U.S. District Court
1843	**Defeated for nomination for Congress**	
1844		Established own law practice with William H. Herndon as junior partner
1846		Elected to Congress
1848	**Lost renomination**	(Chose not to run for Congress, abiding by rule of rotation among Whigs.)
1849	**Rejected for land officer**	Admitted to practice law in U.S. Supreme Court Declined appointment as secretary and then as governor of Oregon Territory

1854	**Defeated for U.S. Senate**	Elected to Illinois state legislature (but declined seat to run for U.S. Senate)
1856	**Defeated for nomination for Vice President**	
1858	**Again defeated for U.S. Senate**	
1860		Elected President

You just read one version of what is referred to as the "List of Lincoln Failures." It is often used to inspire people to overcome life's difficulties using Abraham Lincoln as a model. History professor Lucas Morel compiled this comparison from the Chronology in *Selected Speeches and Writings/Lincoln* by Don E. Fehrenbacher, ed., 1992.

So we are in "bad" company, as they say, in our sin and failures. The good news of the gospel is that we are *supposed* to be in a redeeming process, a reclaiming process, a transformation process, being reconciled to God from sin and death to obedience and eternal life. Consequently, whether you have tried one, or ten, or countless number of times to change your habits, achieve your dreams, live your passion, or just stop yelling at your kids – I want you to know, I need you to know that I believe in you. Give yourself one more chance to break free of doubt, fear, complacency, self-defeating habits, and plain old laziness. Give yourself one more chance to fulfill the hopes of your dreams long since forgotten in a past memory of guilt and despair. It really is quite simple: the quality of your life is the sum total of your choices. Your life today is the result of choices you made yesterday, last month, or even years ago that have long since been forgotten. If you want your life to be different tomorrow, you only need to start making different choices today.

Given the reality of the world today, many of you are living your life on autopilot. You are trying so hard just to survive today you have no time, no energy, no emotional or physical margin, or frankly no interest in learning how to make different choices for a better tomorrow. In this context many of you are simply unaware of the relationship among beliefs, thoughts, emotion, and behavior. Unable or unwilling to take responsibility for our choices we blame shift, procrastinate, and play the role of victim. As you will learn very early in the next section of this book, unless you are willing to develop a focused sense of self-awareness for your life choices, you will continue in a rut and pattern of repeated, self-sabotaging choices of your past. If your current habits are not getting you what you want and your current behavior keeps you under conviction, I suggest that it is time to look for a better way of living your life. You need to discover the peace of walking in the Spirit by bringing your thinking and your behavior in alignment with the Word of God. There you will discover a peace that passes all understanding.

The Pooh Paradox

As a new grandfather I have been reintroduced to the joy of bedtime stories. My daughter always loved the fictional character Winnie-the Pooh, created by A.A. Milne and named after a teddy bear owned by his son, Christopher Robin Milne. The character first appeared in book form in *Winnie-the-Pooh* (1926) and *The House at Pooh Corner* (1928). Once again I have the pleasure of introducing this loveable bear to my grandson, Connor.

In the opening paragraph of *Winnie-the-Pooh*, Christopher Robin, named after Milne's son, and Pooh Bear are coming down the stairs for breakfast with Pooh Bear bumping his head on the stairs. You see, Christopher Robin has Pooh by the ankle, and every day they bump, bump, bump down the stairs. One day Pooh begins to *think* that there has to be a better way of coming down the stairs, bumpity, bumpity, bumpity. At the moment he is just too busy bumping his head to *think* about it. Then he concludes with a sigh of futility that maybe there just isn't a better way of coming down the stairs – so the bumpity, bumpity, bumpity continues. Unfortunately, like many people I know, they keep coming down the stairs the only way they know how hoping there has to be a better way. They keep on doing what they have always done, hoping to get a different result.

Many of you are already falling prey to what I am calling *The Pooh Paradox*, or more technically, unreflective thinking: a form of denial believing that your responses to events or your ineffective habits do not matter, and there is no way to change. You remain trapped in the hope that if you keep doing what you have always done, you will get a different result. This hope has often times been attributed to Albert Einstein as his definition of insanity. The fact remains, and a multiple number of sources attest to the fact, that our habits are perfectly designed to give us the results we get, and our habits are the result of what we believe to be true.

So here is a wake up call - all your habits and choices are formed in belief and thought before you act on them. So if you are not finding meaning, value, and purpose in your life, you must ask yourself if your habits and choices are working for you. Are they adding meaning, value, and purpose to your life? Are they filling your heart with courage or fear? Are you living your dream or frantically seeking to wake up from a nightmare? Are you producing an abundance of fruit in a Spirit led walk of righteous living or vacillating between the tensions of the fleshly desires you were supposed to have died to a long time ago?

Even now you are facing another choice. Your current habits are affecting how you are choosing to respond to what you are reading at this very moment. It does not make any difference if you believe that you have habits that are in motion. Trust me, you do. What is important is that you become aware of those habits and how they control your behavior when you are not thinking about them.

Will you take the opportunity to learn something new or at least be reminded of something you learned in the past? Admit you failed to take action. Close the

knowing and doing gap and commit to taking ownership of your beliefs and habits. Only you can change
the direction of your life. Only you can decide to
stop wishing for a better yesterday and start creating
the reality of a better tomorrow. Possibility *thinking*
today will open the door to impossibility *doing* in
your life for the future. Go find your Bible, and let's
get on the journey together to living the extraordi-
nary life God has planned for you to live.

TRUTH TELLERS

The story is told of Martin Luther who was
suffering in a deep depression. It lasted for quite
some time until his wife confronted him in the midst
of his current behavior. It seems she dressed in black
as if she were preparing to attend a funeral. Martin
Luther noticed her attire and asked her who died.
She simply responded, "God is dead." He admon-
ished her for her blasphemy and asked her why she
would think such a thing. She simply responded to
her despondent husband that he was the one who had
told her God had died – by his behavior.

We all need a truth teller in our lives the way
Luther's wife was able to convey to him the truth of
his behavior. There is a behavioral model called the
Johari window. What this behavior model reveals is
that there are things others know about our behavior
that is unknown to us. This part of the model is called
"the blind zone." We all have a set of behaviors that
we simply do not see. As a result, we need feedback
from a loving and caring partner to help us with what
we do not see. It is far too easy for us to defend and

deny what other truth tellers in our lives are trying to help us see as well. The fact of the matter is that we will always reveal what we really believe to be true simply by the way we act. If you say you believe in God, when are you going to start acting like it? The choice is yours - bumpity, bumpity, bumpity.

Chapter Three

What Do You Really Believe?

*A person will worship something, have no doubt
about that. We may think our tribute is paid in
secret in the dark recesses of our hearts, but it will
come out. That which dominates our imaginations
and our thoughts will determine our lives, and our
character. Therefore, it behooves us to be careful
what we worship, for what we are worshipping we
are becoming. ~Ralph Waldo Emerson*

In the third installment of the Indian Jones movies,
Indiana and his father are in search of the Holy
Grail. Finally reaching the hidden location Indiana
Jones is faced with only one option to save the life
of his father – retrieve the Grail and let his father
drink from the "Cup of Christ." There was one small

problem for Indiana, well three actually. He had to negotiate a series of physical challenges to get to the Grail and then choose the appropriate cup from among hundreds of false ones. The villain tycoon, Donovan, shoots Indiana's father to compel Indiana to retrieve the Grail. He challenges Indiana with this compelling question, "Time to ask yourself (sic), what you do really believe?" You see, up to this point the Grail was only an archaeological relic to Indiana. Now he has to decide whether it has the power to save his father's life. So this is quite a compelling question indeed.

Now I ask you, what do you really believe? The movement from belief to behavior follows a very predictable pattern. Our heart is the seat of our deepest beliefs. What we choose to believe and hide in our hearts links directly in a cause and effect relationship to what and how we choose to think about ourselves, other people, and the events of daily life. These same beliefs and thoughts will create attitudes and emotions that ultimately result in driving our behavior.

In understanding and exploring the relationship among beliefs, thoughts, attitudes, and behavior, we can gain greater self-awareness and ultimately, by cooperating with the Holy Spirit, begin to see great changes take place in our lives.

The Power of Choice

What you choose to believe results in how you choose to behave. The consequences of those choices results in the outcomes of your life events. If you think about your life as a measurement of your understanding of the dynamics of human performance, then you will see that this connection of belief to behavior measures consequences that define the quality of your life. Our behavior is really the constant and consistent revealing of our habits in motion on a daily basis. The peace, joy, and contentment all of us desire in our lives are dependent upon the consequences of our habitual choices.

The relevance and connectivity of belief, to thought, to habits, to outcomes is the root cause for poor human performance at the personal and professional level, namely, the lack of self-awareness. By the term self-awareness I do not mean self-control as discussed previously. Inherent to the sin nature of human beings is the predisposition to yield to body appetites and desires. These desires have their origination in what we call "the flesh" or what we can call here "self." Self-control, in essence, requires you as "self" to control the desires of "self" like the fox guarding the chicken coop. As long as things are running smoothly, self-control appears to work. However, in times of stress, fatigue, temptation, or a real button push, it is really hard to force yourself to act in your own best self-interest. Unless you are convinced to sustain the change and you have some compelling reason to tell your flesh "No" to its desires, your resolve in self-control evaporates in the midst of the stress, fatigue, overwhelming hassles of the day, and your simple desire to satisfy the pleasure craving of your flesh.

What I am talking about in the idea of self-awareness is moving beyond mere self-control. I mean taking personal responsibility for your life and using the principle of accountability to self-manage and regulate your transformation process. The accountability principle is evident throughout the Bible (Gal.6: 7-10). You need someone in your life to keep the power of a compelling vision of transformation a daily focus and provide feedback to your development and progress to the goals you set as part of this process of change.

Every generation has produced a select group of individuals who inspire change and innovation to industry, products, entertainment, and services – our quality of life. They all share a very important and key dynamic in self-awareness. They know what they believe, they know what they think, and they are acutely aware of their habits that drive their performance. The apostle Paul provides for us the Biblical example as to the importance of what we choose to believe that is so prevalent even in the lives of so many who practice Biblical truth without knowing its origin. Paul was very clear that he was pressing toward a specific goal – the perfecting of his heart, mind, and behavior in Christ Jesus, "that I may lay hold of that for which Christ Jesus has also laid hold of me" (Phil 4:12).

Each succeeding generation of innovators as well as a variety of thinkers and authors have discovered and applied this simple truth of behavior; namely, our habits are perfectly designed to get the results they are getting. Habits are patterns of behavior that drive results and consequences of your life choices. Organizational effectiveness coach, Tim Kight, writes in his training manual that we all need to develop self-awareness so we can live with intentionality and know whether our habits are taking us where we want to go. Bestselling author and corporate skills coach, Marshall Goldsmith, also states that the majority of highly successful people have no idea, are unaware of how their behavior is coming across to people who matter –bosses, colleagues, spouses, children, customers, and clients. Goldsmith says that highly successful people live under the superstition that they are successful because of their habits rather than in spite of them. He challenges all of us, and more so, those who are already successful, to constantly ask ourselves, "Is this behavior a legitimate reason for my success, or am I kidding myself?"

So are your habits getting you what you really want out of life? Have you "put on the mind of Christ" to guide your daily life choices? If not it may be time to ask yourself again, "What do you really believe?" Do you believe that you have very few reasons to change your behavior? Regardless of how you judge your level of success or your level of dysfunction, all of us find a host of reasons to stay the course with our current behavior even when we know doing so results in self-defeating and self-sabotaging outcomes and consequences. So why do we resist changing our behavior when we know that doing so is essential to achieving more effective results and outcomes? The simple answer is that change is difficult and changing behavior is even more difficult without some level of appeal to self-interest and compelling, personal desire. For highly successful people who believe in their habits, even destructive ones, the belief in their skills and talent to achieve cloud their awareness to see and change bad habits. Dysfunctional people, who are adept at playing the victim and blame game, purposefully resist becoming self-aware to avoid having to take responsibility for their habits and the outcomes those habits produce.

So now I ask you again, "What do you really believe? The apostle Paul wrote that if you confess with your mouth, Jesus is Lord, and believe in your heart, that God raised Him from the dead, then you shall be saved. The Bible says that out of the abundance of the heart the mouth speaks. The Bible says that "thy Word I have hid in my heart that I might not sin against thee." The word, *believe,* means to cling to, trust in, and rely upon. Are you clinging, trusting, and relying upon Jesus? Your actions speak louder than words. If you say you believe then once again I ask, isn't it time you started behaving like it?

Change Begins With Commitment Not Compliance

Professional change literature and research indicates that you can overcome resistance to change by invoking a natural law principle, namely, discovering the treasure of a person's heart, better known as your motivating self-interest. "For where your treasure is, there will your heart be also" (Matt. 6:21). Interesting how the world again has discovered a natural component of the sin nature in a Biblical truth. Find the source of someone's primary inner drive: pleasure, possessions, power, or prestige, and push that button, and you can effectively begin the change process in any person. Recall the words of Emerson, *"Therefore, it behooves us to be careful what we worship, for what we are worshipping we are becoming."*

Even Jesus had to make a specific appeal to the inner driver of the lame man at the pool of Bethesda (John 5:1-15). *"Do you want to be made well?"* may seem like a strange question to a man who has had the same problem for thirty-eight years, but Jesus asked him the question nonetheless. Interesting that the response of the man does not answer the question, rather he states the reason he believes he is still in his infirmed condition – he has no one to put him into the pool when the water is stirred up. Note again how a false belief drives ineffective behavior and outcomes. There are all kinds of people today stuck in some form of infirmity be it mental, emotional, bad habits, and just plain old bad thinking. Jesus is saying to you – "do you want to be made well?" For both the successful and the dysfunctional, false belief about belief prevents both from changing. The failure to change robs each of us of the opportunity for a better today, a more hopeful tomorrow, and the blessed assurance that Jesus is mine.

To understand how both highly successful people and highly dysfunctional people can share the same belief about changing beliefs, thoughts, and behavior, let's take a look at the dynamics of the three deadly "Ds". There are three common attributes that cause us to stay locked in ineffective habits, and they are denying, defending, and defaming.

Our first reaction to feedback from anyone concerning one of our ineffective habits is denial. Successful people have very few good reasons to change what they believe are habits and behavior that have produced their success. They cannot even entertain the idea that any of their habits could be holding them back and impeding building highly productive and effective relationships at home and at work. Dysfunctional people on the other hand use denial as a means of not having to accept personal responsibility for their lives and the resulting outcomes from years of ineffective and destructive choices.

Denial is simply the voice in our heads that says, "This is not true" to feedback we receive from outside ourselves that regardless of what we are intending, people are experiencing us in exactly the opposite way. Here is another truism of human behavior – people do what they do because there is a pay off to that particular habit or behavior. In all your growing up experiences you accumulated, rated, and acquired beliefs, thoughts, and behaviors (habits) that served your own best interest. These need not be selfish interests but things we think or do to feel safe, to be loved, or to be needed. We become comfortable with what we believe brings some stability in guiding our behavior.

You are what you think, and you do what you believe serves your inner drive and fulfills your own self-interest – you have a master passion of your life, and you worship it. Left unchecked without any sense of self-management on your part and the leading and awareness of the Holy Spirit, you begin to mimic in your behavior the object of your "self-worship." This is your pay-off even if you are misguided in what you believe is behavior that serves your perceived best self-interest. It is also the fundamental issue between keeping your old behavior from a life lived in the flesh and your willingness to die to your "self," to begin walking in a true trusting relationship with the Holy Spirit. When push comes to shove, it is just easier to continue to lapse back into sin and ask forgiveness later than to die to self, submit to God, and pursue a life of excellence and holiness in the nature and character of Jesus Christ. Until a life of excellence in Christ becomes our inner driver, we will continue to trust in and cling to old behaviors even when we know they are not in our best interest and can lead to self-defeating outcomes.

In the world, those self-interests focus around four fundamental drivers mentioned previously: power, prestige, possession and pleasure. You are familiar with these as you lived in one or more of these drivers prior to making your profession of faith to believe in Jesus Christ. The Bible refers to these four drivers as the lust of the eyes, the lust of the flesh, and the boastful pride of life (1 John 2:16). It is interesting to note that people who are successful in the world do not believe they *need* to change their habits once they come to Christ, and people who are dysfunctional in their worldly behavior don't believe they *can* change once they come to Christ. Both of these tendencies reveal how we choose to remain self-centered, self-focused, and even a bit delusional after we come to Christ Jesus. We behave the way we do because we can and believe there is some pay-off to us for doing so. Additionally and for added emphasis – we will continue in this behavior even when we are experiencing painful and self-defeating consequences.

One of the core beliefs you must begin to change in your heart, and we will discuss more of this in a later chapter, is what are you going to choose to be the central driver in your heart? The central theme of this book is that Christians do not fundamentally change in their behavior once they come to Christ because they do not change the fundamental beliefs of their hearts. Where your treasure is your heart will follow. If you still treasure power, possessions, prestige, or pleasure you will continue to struggle with temptation, sin, and the lure to the things of this world.

Paul wrote to the Thessalonians that they were not to be shaken in their faith. He prayed urgently that these new believers would stand fast and firm in the truth of Gospel regardless of persecution or false teachers. He charged Timothy specifically that he was to go to these new believers and establish them and encourage them in their *beliefs* (1 Thess 3:1-3). The ancient Greek word for *shaken* has the connotation of a dog wagging its tail. Who can resist a little puppy, full of exuberance, wagging its tail begging to be cuddled and loved? This is just how Satan will come to tempt you back to a life of sin, sowing seeds of doubt and confusion in your heart and mind. All the while, he is wagging his tail, fawning innocence and affection. He is waiting for you to fall for the bait so he can devour you in your misguided beliefs.

In my military travels, I spent some time in Thailand. I had the occasion to visit a Buddhist monastery during one of my trips. Visitors had the opportunity to pay a small token and release a little bird that was trapped in a cage. By releasing the bird from its cage, you are to vicariously share in the freedom of setting the spirit free. Not a bad word picture to describe how we can be set free from sin. The Lord opens the door to our sinful captivity, and all we need to do is accept the free gift and fly to freedom.

I decided to walk around the monastery and ended up behind the structure where I happened upon some little boys who were monks in training. To my surprise these little fellows had collected up the empty cages and with small pieces of bread were luring the little birds that had just escaped to freedom back into the cages for the next batch of tourists to set them free. What a masterful word picture to describe the cycle of sin and forgiveness in the lives of many Christians. Jesus sets us free and we allow ourselves to be lured back into the cage of sin with tiny morsels of the world's bread crumbs. Unlike these little birds, we are supposed to know better and to want to avoid ever becoming a slave to sin again. Unfortunately, too many Christians do just that – in and out of a cycle of repetitive and habitual sin.

One thing is certain – we cannot make other people change their hearts (the master passion) or change their minds (thinking and attitudes). You have to want to change on your own, and once you trigger the desire to change, God will provide the means to do so. In the flesh there is a natural law to behavior that when we do what we *choose* to do we are committed, but when we do what we *have* to do, we are compliant. Preaching a sermon on the works of the flesh versus the fruit of Spirit has no practical value unless we understand *how* to replace worldly drivers with spiritual drivers. Put in other words, how to move from the world to the Word.

We really do not change behavior over the long term when we are merely being compliant. As soon as whatever pressure making us change dissipates or goes away, we revert back to our old, ineffective, and self-defeating habits. The Corinthians demonstrated this in their behavior when Paul was absent from them. He had to remind them that he was coming back to see them, and they had better get their act together. Even mythological writers have been able to convey the difference between commitment and mere compliance.

In the *Odyssey,* Homer's epic from Greek mythology, we have an example of the difference between commitment and compliance. Odysseus, the main character of the story understands that there is an island of beautiful women (land of the Sirens) who sing a call of pleasure. The purpose of the music is to lure unsuspecting sailors to their death when they choose to follow the irresistible call of the Sirens' lustful song. Odysseus longs to hear the sound of this passionate music. He has his men chain him to the mast of the ship to prevent him from steering them into danger. He also has his men put wax in their ears so they cannot hear the Sirens' fateful song. At times I think we behave like this in our obedience to God. Compliance is the lowest level of obedience and reflects that we still have a heart that is not sold out completely to walking in obedience to the Holy Spirit. A typical southern breakfast begins with bacon and eggs. Two animals are required to provide the ingredients. As they say in the South – the chicken participates and donates the eggs but the pig, well that pig is committed. When you commit your life to Christ, you are supposed to die too.

Another natural law impacting behavior is that when you are aware of the forces that are working to influence your behavior, the greater your ability to choose your response to triggering events. Between any stimuli or event and your response to that event, there is a gap where you are free to choose how to respond. Typically, you can be reactive in response, inactive in your response, or proactive in your response. Why would you make a very difficult situation worse by choosing to respond poorly to that situation? It makes absolutely no sense to do so. A reactive or inactive response will never give you the most optimal outcome. The little known story of Viktor Frankl demonstrates this principle.

Prior to Word War Two, Frankl was a practicing psychiatrist trained in the determinist model and tradition of Sigmund Freud. Determinism has multiple variations of practice and definition to include, causal, biological, environmental, and cultural elements. In its simplest form, determinist of Frankl's time, in the

1930s, believed that events of early childhood shape the personality, behavior, and character of a person for a lifetime. Essentially, there is no free will to choose, and who you are and what you do is merely a byproduct of this early developmental conditioning, and hence the term, *determinism.*

Frankl and his Jewish family were imprisoned in Nazi Germany concentration camps. Except for himself and one sister, his entire family died in these camps or was murdered in the gas chambers. Frankl himself endured multiple tortures and unspeakable degradation and humiliation. He lived day-by-day not knowing life or death.

It was in the midst of this experience that Frankl discovered a unique human capacity that today we call emotional intelligence. Emotional intelligence or EI, is a set of measurable skills and abilities related to self-awareness, self-management, social awareness, and social management. These skills include, but are not limited to, learning the discipline of managing your emotions. In the case of Viktor Frankl, he discovered that rather than simply react and respond to his current situation with hate, he could choose to love. While he suffered greatly in the physical sense, he could be free in his mind and his emotions. This is one thing his captors could not take from him – the freedom to choose his emotions, his response, to their behavior toward him.

It was in discovering the power of this truth that Frankl survived his concentration camp experience. While others died in bitter hatred and resentment, Frankl chose to love the very people responsible for his greatest pain and suffering. Unlike other animals, lacking the capacity to reason and to choose, Frankl demonstrated the fallacy of determinism and reveals unique human capacities to be self-aware and to develop the discipline to manage emotions that lead to high level of personal effectiveness in our life choices.

If you want to change the world for Jesus Christ, a desire that should be alive in the heart of every believer, you eventually have to change your behavior. To change your behavior you will need to begin to change your thinking, and to change your thinking, you will have to change the core beliefs and values of your heart. This is true spiritual alignment that is fundamental to the transformation process of *metamorphosis*. So now is the time to ask you again, "what do you really believe?" Given that you have confessed with your mouth and believe (cling to, trust in, rely upon, surrender the totality of your personality and behavior preferences) in your heart that Jesus is Lord and was raised from the dead, don't you think it is time to begin learning how to act like it?

Part Two

The Process Of Transformation

Chapter Four

Back To the Basics

"We will pursue perfection. We will no doubt not achieve perfection, but in the pursuit of perfection, we will achieve excellence."
~Vince Lombardi

There is no doubt that the reason so many Christians struggle in their walk in the Spirit is that they lack the fundamental understanding of the basics of the gospel. In my teaching and travels, I never cease to be amazed at how many faithful church attendees lack a fundamental knowledge of even the most basic Bible stories. Is it any wonder that we have believers struggling with sin issues that should be non-negotiable, and they continue to recycle in self-destructive behaviors because they are ignorant of what the Bible has to say about sin, salvation, redemption, sanctification and reconciliation? The main problem for Christians in America is a failure of church leadership to stay grounded in the truth of the Bible. We have, as Jesus told John, become like the church at Ephesus and have lost our first love. Beyond that, we have become like the church at Thyatira, reluctant and unwilling to confront the sin of tolerance and every form of ungodliness. We have become corrupt in church practice all the while claiming to be moving beyond the so-called outdated and fundamental doctrines of biblical truth.

I have fun with the Lombardi quotation in my professional development seminars. I tease folks by stating that he was another great Italian-American making the illusion that I am the other great Italian-American. We share not only heritage and ethnicity but the same passion for excellence. If you know the history of the Green Bay Packers during the Lombardi era, then you know that, while not achieving perfection, they did obtain excellence. Of their remarkable accomplishments, three consecutive world championships remain unmatched in the history of the National Football League.

Lombardi's genius was demonstrated in many ways, but the one that his players appreciated the most was the way he reduced each play down to its basic elements. So too, the apostle Paul, in his pursuit of excellence in the gospel, reduces each aspect of the Christian walk of faith into fundamental elements. One story told of Lombardi at his first team meeting centers on his passion and the power of his speech to the team. He reminded these men that he had never been a loser, and he did not intend on starting with them. In his first team meeting, Lombardi told his players they were going to get back to basics, and he held up a football to them stating, "Gentlemen, this is a football." You cannot get any more basic than that, can you? Later, Lombardi confided to one of his key players that he was concerned the whole team might leave town as a result of that introductory speech. Well they hung around, bought into Lombardi's passion for excellence, and the rest is history as they say.

I wonder if the apostle Paul was ever concerned about how many Corinthians might stick around after hearing his "team meeting" letter read to them by one of their elders. Your own study of the Bible should indicate to you that Paul had no desire to soften the message of sin, repentance, redemption, reconciliation, and death-to-the-flesh-life-in-the-Spirit teaching. Paul, like Lombardi, had no interest in being a loser. Lombardi challenged his team regarding their level of commitment and desire. "I'm going to find thirty-six men who have the pride to make any sacrifice to win."

Paul also had his eye on perfection, and he was looking for any man or woman, slave or free, Jew or Gentile, to sacrifice to win the prize of the upward call of Christ. Have you checked your commitment level lately? We need to get back to basics making sure we understand what it is about ourselves that needs to change once we come to a profession of faith in the Lord Jesus. Paul exhorted the believers in Rome to cast off the works of darkness and put on the armor of light. "Let us walk properly, in excellence, as in the day, and not in revelry, and drunkenness, not in lewdness and lust, not in strife and envy" (Romans

13:12-14). We need to understand what it will take in our own behavior to win, to excel, to claim our prize in Christ, and hear our heavenly Father say, "well done thy good and faithful servant." We need to understand that we must put on Jesus Christ and make no provision for the flesh to fulfill its lusts. Let's go for it!

What Does It Mean to Be a Christian?

The main problem for the authentic Christian, in the transformation process from sinner to saint, is the struggle that is encountered due to the lack of proper understanding of our identity in Jesus Christ. Even the word *Christian* has lost clarity of meaning and is a very vague term in the culture of America today. If you were to live in India, China, or a Muslim country and called yourself a Christian, the people in those countries would know exactly what you mean. Not so here in the United States where the word *Christian* has no specific connotation and no specific reference point. The word has lost its relevance and significance short of some clarification and context. In the midst of this confusion, it is possible for us, as authentic Christians in America, to lose our true identity in Christ and consequently lose a sense of what transforms us into His image.

By authentic Christian I mean those who adhere to the fundamentals of the Bible regarding, sin, salvation, the virgin birth, the deity of Jesus Christ, the resurrection of the dead, reconciliation to God the Father through faith in His only begotten Son, Jesus Christ. What I mean by authentic Christian is described by the apostle Paul in all of his New Testament writings.

Followers of Jesus were "first called Christians in Antioch" (Acts 11:26). The word itself, *Christian*, meaning a follower of Christ or "little Christ," is only used three times in the New Testament. The intent of its use is speculative. Perhaps it was used as a derogatory term to identify Jews who were believers in Jesus as Messiah. Perhaps it was a more general reference to those who were also of "the Way" pertaining to Jesus' reference as "the Way, the Truth, and the Life." While the use of the term may be in doubt, what is not in doubt is what it meant to be a follower of Jesus regardless of the label ascribed to you in a Biblical context.

In the transformation process model that will follow, conviction begins the first step in the process in the act of repentance, by the preaching of the Word. There are a lot of people who have a belief in Jesus Christ as a mere historical figure and Christianity as a body of creeds and doctrines that comprise a world religion. What these people do not have is the heart-felt conviction that Jesus Christ is God incarnate – God in the flesh. Essential to authentic Christianity is the conviction that Jesus Christ is God, who came to the earth in bodily form, in real flesh, who died, was buried, and resurrected bodily as the Savior of the world. The purpose of His death and resurrection was to make a complete atonement for the sin of Adam and all past and future sin of the world so that anyone who would be convicted to believe (cling to, trust in, and rely upon, giving up all claim to their own identity and personality) in Jesus would not perish but have everlasting life.

This contrast, from mere mental assent or mental acknowledgement of historical fact and a spiritual awakening where you die to self so you may be resurrected in Christ, starts with conviction. If you read Acts 26, you will see how this process of acknowledgement versus conviction plays out between Paul and King Agrippa and its outcome as compared to John 4 with Jesus and the woman at the well in Samaria. Please note two key aspects of these conversations, Paul with King Agrippa and Jesus with the Samaritan woman. In both accounts, you will see Jesus and Paul making a personal connection to the mental knowledge of their counterparts in the conversation. Second, you will see that the fundamental purpose of both conversations is not merely to have a debate about religious history and doctrine or how to develop a strategy for solving world hunger or the current leprosy crisis, but to transform the heart of the listener through the power of the Word to create a salvation experience and begin the journey of spiritual transformation.

In the account of John 4, Jesus creates a common focus of conversation around water and creates an emotional, compelling word picture of the immediate need of the woman for water and His ability to quench her spiritual thirst. Note too how Paul appeals to King Agrippa's knowledge of the prophets and makes an intellectual appeal to then create an emotional response to Agrippa's own spiritual hunger. Jesus revealed himself in very clear and simple terms to the Samaritan woman, and Paul challenged Agrippa with logic and reason that was irrefutable in the truth of the Jewish scriptures. The woman at the well, along with many of her Samaritan brethren, ends up believing in Jesus as their Savior. Unfortunately, King Agrippa did not make a choice for Christ during this encounter with Paul. He admits that Paul almost persuaded him to become a Christian. He was convinced of the argument, but sadly, not convicted in his heart.

To be an authentic Christian you have to identify with and enter into the death, burial, and resurrection of Jesus Christ. C.S. Lewis explained that "in Christ a new kind of man appeared: and the new kind of life which began in Him is to be put into us." This new life is not just a mental acknowledgement or even the persuasion of mental logic and argument. To be "in Christ" is to be converted by the power of the Holy Spirit with conviction in your heart that Jesus Christ is the Son of God, Savior of the World, and Lord of your life. To be "in Christ" means to know Him as He is revealed in the Word of God, the Holy Bible, and to spend time developing a personal relationship with Him.

In seeking to understand what it means as a Christian to have a personal relationship with Jesus, consider the words of Juan Carlos Ortiz who writes,

"We need a new generation of Christians who know that the church is centered around a Person who lives within them. Jesus didn't leave us with just a book and tell us, 'I leave the Bible. Try to find out all you can from it by making concordances and commentaries.' No, He didn't say that. 'Lo, I am with you always,' He promised. 'I'm not leaving you with a book alone. I am there, in your hearts.' ...We just have to know that we have the Author of the book within us..."

The apostle Paul wrote to the believers in Ephesus that we were chosen *in* Jesus Christ (Eph. 1:4). He goes on to say that in Him we have redemption through His blood and the forgiveness of sins (1:7). This first chapter of Ephesians is loaded with continuous references to "in Him, by Him, through Him." Then Paul provides a glorious prayer that our eyes, the eyes of our hearts (conviction), would be open to receive this spiritual wisdom that by accepting the work of the cross and believing in Jesus Christ, we would be redeemed, reconciled, and at peace with God. Adrian Rogers provides a simple reminder of what this personal relationship in Christ looks like when he wrote:

"Are you converted to Christ? Are you committed to Christ? Are you crucified with Christ? Has there been a persuasion? Is there a profession? And is there a persecution? These are the true marks of a Christian."

The hallmark of any relationship is love. Our personal relationship with Jesus Christ is grounded on God the Father's love for us. The Bible says that while we were yet sinners, separated from God, at war with God, He sent His Son to die for us. Paul writes that not only did He die for us, but that His death was as a substitute for our guilt and condemnation. In His death we have the opportunity for eternal life (Col. 2). Not only are we forgiven, but this same Bible passage says the handwriting of our guilty sentences has been removed, taken away, lost forever. By entering into this personal relationship with Jesus Christ, we are no longer under the curse and sentence of a death penalty, but we have been pardoned, set free to a life in Christ. Not only are we now alive in Christ but we have meaning, value, and purpose for our life in a God ordained calling to ministry in service to our King Jesus. You can hear the chorus of saints singing, "blessed assurance, Jesus is mine – oh what a foretaste of glory divine."

There is a warning; however we must be on guard, for just as there has always been a false promise of excellence without the effort, so too, there has always been a false promise of salvation without the cross. Regardless of recent polls suggesting that 57% of so-called American Evangelicals are willing to concede other paths to salvation than Jesus, that is not what the Bible says. In fact, to believe that there are alternatives to salvation other than the cross of Christ is to discount the truth of the Bible. When you give up on the Biblical fundamental that "Jesus is The Way, and The Truth, and The Life, and no one can come to the Father but by Him," you have lost the gospel.

Paul wrote too that we are to be on guard against false teachers. He did not take a passive stand against those who were willing to spread a false doctrine and a false Christ. Paul's influence as an apostle was constantly under attack from false teachers, and he knew the risk of converts shifting their attention from the influence of the Holy Spirit that was working through Paul, to those with a more flattering speech and a flesh accommodating gospel. We have such false teachers among us today making promises of health, wealth, and material prosperity. These false teachers pander a message of the abundant life in material things and pursuing excellence, not in biblical conduct and behavior, but in condos, cars and a life of material affluence. That might be appealing as a false gospel in America, but that "dog won't hunt," as they say in the South, for Christians suffering persecution for the name of Christ in India, China, and Muslim countries around the world.

We are not immune from this same corruption of the gospel today. Sadly, at least for Christianity in America, we are more willing to accommodate the notion of tolerance as the only absolute value, discarding centuries of historical and timeless principles to guide our behavior. Doing so will sadly lead many to death and destruction. The apostle Paul warned against the foolish wisdom of this world. Tragically, if this poll is accurate at all, the desire for open mindedness will ultimately lead to our brains falling out. Once you leave the fundamentals, you leave the opportunity for being grounded in the very principles necessary for excellence and walking in the truth of the gospel.

As you move into the next chapter, you will discover the pathway to excellence in Christ that will keep you grounded and guarded against false belief. As you learn and apply this process every day, you will begin to develop the discipline of living your life in Christ and not for your passions and desires of this fallen world. To whom the Lord sets free is free in deed. You need to begin to consider learning how to *be* in your character and *behave* in your conduct as an authentic Christian. Learning requires knowledge, understanding, and a change of behavior.

Oswald Chambers wrote in his devotional, *My Utmost for His Highest*, the following:

> To become one with Jesus Christ, a person must be willing not only to give up sin but also to surrender ones whole way of looking at things. Being born again by the Spirit of God means that we must first be willing to let go before we can grasp something else. . . . When people really see themselves as the Lord sees them, it is not the terribly offensive sins of the flesh that shock them but the awful nature of pride of their own hearts opposing Jesus Christ.

Unless we surrender our entire self to Jesus Christ, we will never reach a place where we can begin a transformation from a life lived in the nature of Adam, to a life lived in the Spirit of Jesus Christ. Having a desire to live godly is not enough. It is God's desire to restore us back to the original creation, into His image. His desire is for us to be holy as He is holy (1 Peter 1:16). Metamorphosis is the Word of God and the Spirit of God working together to complete our restoration into the image, nature, and behavior of His Son, Jesus Christ. With the Word of God planted deep into your heart, you can begin your transformation process into the image of Jesus Christ. So, I ask you again. If you claim to be a Christian isn't it time you started acting like it?

Chapter Five

The Process for Renewal and Transformation

It's only when we truly know and understand that we have a limited time on earth — and that we have no way of knowing when our time is up, we will then begin to live each day to the fullest, as if it was the only one we had. ~Dr. Elizabeth Kubler-Ross

I have worked in healthcare my entire adult life. Serving over twenty years in the United States Army Medical Department, I began my civilian healthcare career as a clinical administrative director, and currently develop and present seminars in organizational development for hospital leadership and their employees. I have shared in the mixed experiences of being present with patients and family at both the beginning and the end of physical life. Being in the presence of a person taking their last breath is a humbling and extremely profound experience. Oddly, it is in the presence of death that we are often drawn so powerfully to examine how we actually lived – did our life on earth matter. Did my life count for something? Did my life have meaning, value, and purpose?

In my experiences of helping families bring closure to the death of a loved one, I have been bewildered by the stark contrast in conversations that take place in these final moments of life. As you can imagine there are often strong and conflicting emotions at times of medical crisis. If you have had personal experiences of your own with the passing of a family member or close friend, you understand what these moments can be like. Ironically, most of these discussions from both families and the patients themselves are not so much about the fear of death but the fear that tragically they had somehow missed out on living life. They seem overwhelmed by the gross reality that it may take dying for any of us to awaken to the realization that we may not be really living a life of meaning and purpose.

In the movie, *Saving Private Ryan*, we are held awe struck, riveted to the steely eyes of an elderly man staring through a grave marker at Normandy beach in France with laser like focus. With a piercing gaze and tear-filled eyes, he asks his wife, "Did I live my life well?" In the final words of life from a man who dies so Ryan might live, we hear this plea, "Earn this and live your life well." The plea is for Ryan not to waste his life on the sacrifice of the men, who died so courageously, that he might return home the sole survivor of four brothers at war. Live well Private Ryan, live well. Do not let our death for your life be in vain.

The journey of living our life well in Christ begins ironically with our own death. Not that we actually die physically, but that we put the desires of our flesh man to death and purpose to live in our "spirit man" in Christ. The apostle Paul writes of this struggle between our flesh and spirit in his letters to the Asian churches birthed in his missionary travels. Many years earlier, the Greek philosopher Aristotle also identified with this very struggle, "I count him braver who overcomes his desires than him who overcomes his enemies; for the hardest victory is the victory over self." Victory over self seems to be at the very heart of our transformation process. The apostle Paul conveys the condition of his heart in the letter to the Romans concerning how he struggled with the flesh during his own transformation experience.

> For we know that the law is spiritual: but I am carnal, sold under sin. For that which I do I allow not: for what I would, that do I not; but what I hate, that do I. If then I do that which I would not, I consent unto the law that it is good. Now then it is no more I that do it, but sin that dwelleth in me. For I know that in me (that is, in my flesh,) dwelleth no good

thing: for to will is present with me; but how to perform that which is good I find not. For the good that I would I do not: but the evil which I would not, that I do. Now if I do that I would not, it is no more I that do it, but sin that dwelleth in me. I find then a law, that, when I would do good, evil is present with me. (Romans 7:14-21)

How to perform that which is good? Now that is the real question, is it not?

Living your life well in Christ begins with dying. Just as we read in the words of Kubler-Ross, renowned grief expert, "knowing we have limited time," we get to make a choice to live for *self* or give up our lives to live for Christ. Jesus also sacrificed and died so that we might live and that our lives might count for something more than simply seeking power, prestige, pleasure, and possessions of this world. There is an irony in living and dying in that the more you seek to live this life, the more you are really dying. The more you seek to lose your life, then and only then, do you truly discover your real life in Jesus Christ.

In his book *Your Inner CEO: Unleash the Executive Within*, executive coach Allan Cox writes, "By the time executives get married, take on a mortgage, raise the kids, cope with the crabgrass, climb the corporate ladder, do their best to manage career pressures, build their net worth, and get into their 40s, they have lost touch with what they believe in and care about most deeply." What an indictment of living for the things of this world only to discover that they do not satisfy. Author and executive coach Stephen R. Covey wrote in *7 Habits of Highly Effective People* way back in 1989 that people are climbing corporate ladders only to get to the top and discover the ladders are leaning against the wrong walls.

Viktor Frankl, whom we met in an earlier chapter, wrote of his new insights and beliefs following his torturous experiences in his book, *Man's Search for Meaning*. Frankl argues against his mentor, Sigmund Freud, and other existential philosophers that human beings are born into this world with a purpose. Frankl is correct in his assertion. By putting this belief into practice, his survival experience is a testament to living with the power of purpose in one's life. He misidentifies, however, the real purpose of our lives as the creation of fulfilling work and meaningful relationships with other people. As motivating as these might be to adding purpose to our lives, our real purpose in life is to die to self and to reconcile with our heavenly Father so that we are reunited in His love and creation. Then in our own transformation experience, go out into the world and lead others back to peace with their heavenly Father.

Jesus said that the truth shall make us free, but what is truth? Truth is the revelation of the Word of God in the Bible. The Bible is the life blood of the authentic Christian. The Bible is the Word of God, and God is His Word. The key to living a victorious Christian life is to find meaning, value, and purpose for your life by discovering what the Word of God says, understanding what the Word of God means, and then living the Word of God as you apply its truth in your daily life choices and behavior.

The Power of the Resurrection

The apostle Paul gives us a clear understanding that our power in life, the power of personal change and transformation is directly linked to self-denial and surrendering to the Lordship of Jesus Christ. In Colossians 1:4-8, Paul reveals that faith in Christ through the love of the saints, heard in the word of the truth of the gospel, is a necessary and sufficient condition to eternal life. Then Paul goes on to say, "He has delivered us from the power of darkness and conveyed *us* into the kingdom of the Son of His love, in whom we have redemption through His blood, the forgiveness of sins" (Col 1:12-14). Then in chapter two Paul tells us that having received Christ we are to be rooted, established, and built up in Jesus Christ. Jesus is pre-eminent over all creation, the first of all things even unto death. "For in Him dwells all the fullness of the Godhead bodily; and you are complete in Him, who is the head of all principality and power" (Col 2: 9-10).

In a comparable chapter in the letter to the Philippians, Paul tells us how the power of the resurrection explicitly provides us the resource to live in our transformation experience with Christ. The power of the resurrection is the power that supplies us with the struggle of breaking free from a life of sin and propels us into a walk of obedience in the Spirit.

"That I may know Him and the power of His resurrection, and the fellowship of His sufferings, being conformed to His death, if, by any means, I may attain to the resurrection from the dead (Phil 3: 10-11)."

Breaking free from a life of sin, propelled into a walk of obedience is the promise of the power of God in you. If you have received Jesus Christ and have been raised up with Him in power, can you tell me why you are living your life in a lack of spiritual abundance? Can it be that you have been robbed of this blessing? Paul warned the Colossians specifically not to be cheated through worldly philosophy and deceit (Col 2:8). If Allan Cox tells us anything of his corporate American world, it is the discovery that he finds business executives cheated of life's true meaning and purpose continually. Are you being cheated? Are you being deceived in a pursuit of worldly power? If you are claiming to be an authentic Christian ask yourself, "Are you living your life well?"

This struggle to transform from a life of the flesh to a life in the Spirit is available to anyone who is *willing* to pursue it. Paul describes that this struggle of wanting to do good requires both the will and the knowledge to do so. I can give you the knowledge in this book. I can identify for you the process of moving from worldly behavior to Christ like behavior. What you believe, how you think, and the way you choose to manage your behavior, will stay the same unless you are willing to change. Sadly, many people are choosing not to love God, but instead, choosing to hang onto a life of pleasure and serving self rather than choosing to surrender to a life of obedience in Jesus Christ. There is no way to live a satisfied life outside of a loving relationship with Jesus Christ. We were made by God for His pleasure. Jesus Christ came to this world to provide us the means of restoring a personal, loving relationship with God. We must enter into the death of Jesus Christ to enter into His resurrection. Creating the means for us to be reconciled to the Father was the purpose of His coming. There is no other way to the Father but by His Son. There is no short cut to salvation. There is no short cut to spiritual transformation either. It must come by way of the struggle and crucible of the cocoon in the power of the resurrection.

Chapter Six

The Living and Dying Distinction

We are not human beings having a spiritual experience. We are spiritual beings having a human experience. – Teilhard de Chardin

If we stop and think about what life is really about, we see clearly that it has less to do with what we might call physical life and far more to do with what we might call spiritual life. This distinction is very clear when you look at people living in absolute luxury of the physical aspects of life yet who are so emotionally and spiritually wretched. Likewise, we have seen countless examples of people who live in the midst of physical and material need, total abject poverty, and yet live in a life of spiritual contentment.

I had first hand evidence of this remarkable truth in my travels to India and time spent with some of the nuns who were at the time fulfilling the work of Mother Theresa. They shared a story with me regarding a British documentary film team who traveled to India to chronicle the work of Mother Theresa. Following her one morning into the streets filled with the outcasts and the suffering, the crew filmed Mother Theresa caring for a man with open and oozing sores all over his body. On her hands and knees, tenderly expressing the love of Christ, she attended to the physical suffering of this man. The camera man was moved, not with compassion, but with his own revulsion, and he was overheard by Mother Theresa saying, "There is not enough money in the world to pay me to do what that woman is doing." Mother Theresa looked up from where she was kneeling and kindly replied to the young man, "It's all right – because there is not enough money in the world to pay me to do it either."

Clearly, real living is not about what you have or do not have in the physical and material sense but about a mindset, a perspective of discovering meaning, value, and purpose in whom you are in Christ and what you choose to do with your life. As we read in the very beginning of this book, your life is the sum product of your choosing. That being the case, how can we be assured that we are choosing wisely, effectively and in ways that add meaning, value and purpose to a life lived well? The answer is in the transformation pathway I have named C4.

C4 is the name of the process for you to identify with and engage in the necessary behavior to live an abundant life in Christ. C4 is a tool to help you continuously build and sustain the necessary alignment between what the Bible teaches as truth, what you *believe* about what the Bible teaches, how you choose to *think* about what you believe, how you *respond* emotionally to your beliefs, and ultimately how to choose to *behave* based on your attitudes and habits that follow your thinking. I know this sounds very complex at the moment but trust me, once you make the causal connections between the Bible, your thinking, and your behavior choices, you will discover the beauty and simplicity of C4 to guide you to excellence in your Christian walk and metamorphosis process.

Remember there is no magic wand in spiritual growth. There is no magic pill you swallow to die to the lust of your flesh and deny yourself so you can enter into oneness of fellowship with Jesus Christ. The Holy Spirit will not impose Himself on us either – making us little obedient robots. We must live out our new life in Christ by yielding to the Holy Spirit who will lead and guide us. To do otherwise would take away from the value of freely choosing to walk in a more excellent way in the Spirit. You choose to live in Christ and die to self. This knowledge and understanding, chosen with effective behavior that aligns to Biblical truth, really identifies someone as an authentic Christian.

This transformation process is something you must commit to daily. You must daily learn to die to self and the flesh and walk in obedience. You must be moving forward in your walk with Christ constantly. General George Patton was well known for his military strategy of attack, attack, attack; He knew that being on the offensive was the only strategy to ensure victory in warfare. Attacking gives you the greatest opportunity of maintaining the momentum of the battlefield, confusing the enemy, and gaining ground toward the ultimate objective. In the power of the resurrection and the leading of the Holy Spirit, we must be advancing constantly in our growth and transformation from a life lived serving self, to a life lived serving our Lord and Savior Jesus Christ.

I know that Christians become skeptical when they hear or read about what we must do to participate in our sanctification process. The concern, referring to the notion of a "works" oriented theology, while legitimate with regards to salvation, is off base when it comes to our walk in the Spirit. Lazy thinking can lead to lazy behavior. Negative thinking can lead to negative behavior. Self-centered thinking can lead to self-centered behavior. The simple truth is that God uses a process, a mechanical process. The born again experience is followed by a lifelong process committed to molding, shaping, and conforming into the image and character of Jesus Christ, and it requires your active participation.

Do not confuse your active participation in this growth and maturation process with using your own power or doing a spiritual work in the flesh. We are saved by God's grace, and we are transformed by God's power. The evidence of your transformation is supposed to be visible by how you behave. The Bible calls this evidence the fruit of the Spirit (Gal 5:22-23). The apostle Paul contrasts this transformation character of the Spirit with the works of the flesh. When you yield your life over to the Holy Spirit, you will begin to produce in your behavior the outward evidence of your spiritual transformation: love, joy, peace, patience, kindness, goodness, faithfulness, gentleness, and self-control. Contrast this list to the works of the flesh: adultery, fornication, uncleanness, morbid sexual desire, idolatry, witchcraft, hatred, wrath, strife, heresy, envy, murders, drunkenness, wild partying. Note that the Bible says that those who are habitual in the practice of the works of the flesh will not inherit the kingdom of God. Now there are a lot of important passages in the Bible, but when there is a passage that says," if you do these things, you will not inherit the Kingdom of God," then we better be paying attention.

In my professional development seminars, the focus is creating organizational excellence by maximizing individual performance; I often do an exercise with the participants where I ask them to describe in one word attributes their description of what the ideal boss and ideal coworker would look like in their behaviors. We start by developing the list word by word, and invariably the list is almost always identical and includes the following for both the "ideal" boss and the "ideal" coworker: trustworthy, honest, kind, compassionate, friendly, team player, courteous, caring, role model, good listener, accountable, positive, enthusiastic, competent, and committed. I have probably conducted this little exercise in over 100 groups in various parts of the country, and the list is virtually identical every time. Now if you care to compare this list with the list of behaviors that compile the fruit of the Spirit, you will find, amazingly, a near one to one correlation. The only word missing is love, and if you take all these other words together to summarize them in one word, it would be *love* as a verb not a noun.

I was speaking recently at a large gathering of healthcare executives, physicians, and nurses at a leadership summit conference. I was speaking, of course, on individual behavior competencies that drive organizational performance excellence. During my presentation, a nurse began to complain quite profusely that the only problem with behavior in healthcare belonged to the doctors. While this is somewhat of an accurate statement, she failed to see that, in her sarcasm and negativity, she was reflecting the very behavior that she was so vehemently condemning.

Letting her continue her ranting for a few moments, I gently asked her to reconsider her statements given that there were likely doctors in the audience. I then asked for a show of hands to see how many physicians were in attendance. A significant number of hands went into the air. In an attempt to calm their hurt feelings and anger over these strong statements, I proceeded by telling the group what I thought everyone who works in healthcare needs – a big hug. I spoke to how people in healthcare give out so much of themselves in love and compassion to others and then are neglected in getting any love in return.

When I completed my presentation, a small line of participants formed in front of me to ask questions and receive my business card. One woman approached with hesitation and started to ask a question and then paused, her eyes averting direct contact with mine. Before she could begin speaking again, I asked her if she wanted a hug. She looked up at me, a big grin on her face and responded with an emphatic "YES!"

Doing *love* - the verb - to others becomes a part of who you are in your spiritual transformation. Notice that to do love, you make a choice. "Here we go again," I can hear you saying. Well everything about what we do is always a matter of choice – even to love. So we have a choice to walk in the Spirit or walk in the flesh. We have a choice to be self-centered or in love, focus on the legitimate needs of others. Your own identity as an authentic Christian is directly reflected in your capacity and choice to love others. Jesus said himself in John 13:35, "By this shall all men know that ye are my disciples, if ye have love one to another."

You see our transformation process is not only for our benefit and essential to our own effectiveness in our Christian walk, but it is essential in our relationship to other believers in the body of Christ. Transformational love is not a feeling or an impulse but a willful choice in the power of the Holy Spirit. Otherwise, how could you possibly be able to forgive anyone who committed an act of harm against you?

Forgiveness is an act of love, and love is a choice in the power of the Spirit of God. Your daily life is most likely going to be full of encounters with people you do not like or care to be around – most likely people at your work. Ask them what they want from you as a coworker, and you will find all they really want is for you to *do* love to them in your behavior.

That little exercise I exposed you to earlier has a hook in it. Every time I conclude that exercise with seminar participants and I let them talk about and identify all the people they work with that do not demonstrate those loving qualities, I then turn on them and ask how many of them behave in the manner they desire in the behavior of others? That is when heads begin to drop, and you can see guilt begin to set in on their faces. How easy it is for us to demand that others treat us with respect, kindness, caring, compassion – treat us in love. Quite another story when that is the expectation for our own behavior. Remember the word repent that we spoke about earlier? This might be a good time for you to consider changing your mind about your own heart, your own thinking, and your own behavior concerning the fruit of the Spirit and the works of the flesh. According to the Word of God, your eternal destiny is at stake in that choice – so choose wisely.

Chapter Seven

The Transformation Process

Get alone with Jesus and either tell Him that you do not want sin to die out in you - or else tell Him that at all costs you want to be identified with His death. ~Oswald Chambers

The transformation process, our metamorphosis, is supposed to take us from a life lived in the flesh, our carnal minds, to a life lived in the Spirit, our spiritual minds (Romans 8:5-11). Gaining a biblical perspective of how the mind works and functions will be essential to your understanding how to break free of worldly habits that are holding you back in your spiritual development. These habits are not just holding you back from growing in Christ; these habits are keeping you bound in sin that is keeping you separated from the rich, full, personal relationship you are to enjoy with your heavenly Father.

Jesus wrote (John 15:1-8) that we are to abide *in* Him and *in* the Father. We are to be living an abundant life *in* Christ. That means we are not only to be saved from our sins, but we are to be productive in the ministry to others. The word *abide* has the meaning of dwelling in – like pitching a tent in Jesus. So if you have built your home in Christ, why do you worry; why do you fret; why do you complain; why do you whine; why do you act like a victim of your circumstances? Why? The answer is that you might have started into your Christian experience with the wrong motive or a misunderstanding of the nature of a personal relationship with Jesus Christ. Regardless, as you are about to see now, we are going to change that for you by letting you begin this process over again. We are going back to the basics to discover the fundamental principles of the spiritual transformation that will lead us to an abundant life in Jesus Christ.

The apostle Paul outlines four fundamental steps to a life being reborn and renewed into the glorious image of our Lord and Savior Jesus Christ. He wrote, in conditional sentence structure, that *if* we have been raised with Christ, we are to be seeking those things which are spiritual, not the things of the flesh (Col 3:1-11). We are to put to death "flesh thinking" and "flesh habits." We do not do that until we first have a change of heart, "for where your treasure is there your heart will be also" (Matt. 6:21). Unless you have changed your desires from the things of this world and

114

made Jesus your treasure, any hope of long lasting, sustained change in your thinking and behavior are doomed. There is not enough *self*-control or *self*-will or behavior modification for you to endure the sustained discomfort of telling yourself "no" to the desires of your flesh. That is the reason worldly thinking, or so-called self-help techniques, fail to bring sustained and permanent change of behavior in the lives of Christians who lack an understanding of the spiritual transformation process. Remember your flesh is not your friend, and you cannot do a work in the Spirit by worldly or fleshly effort.

Having said this, I do not mean for you to assume that there is not a certain amount of effort, good old fashioned hard work that authentic Christians need to apply to their lives to conform to the nature and character of Jesus Christ. The apostle Paul provides for us a biblical model for this authentic Christian character, "And not only so, but we glory in tribulations also: knowing that tribulation works patience; and patience, experience; and experience, hope" (Romans 5:3-4). All of us, when we receive Jesus as personal Savior begin a growing and maturation process. This process includes establishing and building your Christian character to conform to the nature and character of Jesus. The Bible says in Philippians 1:6, ". . . He which hath begun a good work in you will perform it. . ." When you are saved, God simply begins a good work in you. You are God's handiwork, and He will be faithful to complete the work He has begun in you, and that work predominantly is to complete His will in your life – your sanctification, your holy transformation into the nature and character of His Son, Jesus (1Thess. 4:3).

It bears repeating that what you believe to be true in your heart and in your mind drives the choices that result in your behavior. You cannot have a divided heart, one part wanting to commit to and serve the Lord Jesus and the other part wanting to seek after the pleasures and the lure of the things of the flesh. The first belief that needs to change, that you must change, to have a successful heart transformation is a shift from being a victim and playing the blame game, to accepting and taking full responsibility and accountability for your own life and the choices you make in your life. It is fundamental and absolutely essential for you to believe without a shadow of a doubt that you have the freedom and capacity of choice, and your best life in Christ is a direct result of you choosing wisely.

My first job leaving the military, I served as the administrative director for surgical services in a hospital where I had direct responsibility over the open heart surgery program. Patients with coronary artery disease face a severe medical crisis. Often times this crisis is the direct result of poor life choices. Bad eating habits, over weight, cigarette smoking, excessive use of drugs and alcohol, and little or no exercise are all risk factors that can lead to heart disease that ultimately requires coronary artery bypass surgery to save a person's life.

Time and again I have witnessed families in the midst of a crisis. Their loved one has survived a surgical procedure and has been given a second chance at life. These patients receive a host of education on diet, exercise, smoking cessation, and weight control. Virtually every patient expresses a deep sense of gratitude and relief at a fresh start in life. They all begin their new life with great expectation and promises of all the life changes they are going to make so they do not have to suffer the consequences of poor life choices again. Unfortunately, medical studies indicate that less than 30% of the patients who have open heart surgery change their habits in a way that will make a significant difference in their overall health for the future. Many of them even begin to start smoking again and relatively few sustain their cardiovascular exercise programs. Even with appropriate education and with the memory of a near fatal medical crisis, it is a simple fact that adults simply do not change their behavior easily even when it is in their own best self-interest to do so.

Why is it so hard for us to change our habits even when we know that failing to change our habits can be the direct cause of our death – both physical and spiritual death? Why is it that intelligent people can choose to behave in such irrational ways knowing in advance that the outcomes of those choices can only lead to pain, sorrow, suffering, and tragedy in their lives? Providing you the answer to this fundamental question is precisely why I have written this book. Consequently, this book can be the beginning of a real turning point in your life. We are reaching the place now in your reading where I am about to reveal to you the mechanics of your habits and choices and how you can actually control your response to any event with the greatest opportunity for improved outcomes and blessings in your life. You must decide now to believe that change is possible. You must believe that you are capable of change. You must commit to doing the hard work to change and by appropriating the power of the Holy Spirit in your life; you will ultimately improve your spiritual relationship with God and your family. By making this choice, you will ultimately begin living a life of spiritual abundance that God has intended for you all along.

The Bible is full of many promises for you. A belief that is absolutely essential for you to place in your heart is that not only *can* you change but when you seek God with all your heart, you will find Him, and you *will* change. The Bible says in Jeremiah 29-13, "You will seek me and find me, when you seek me with all your heart. I will be found by you declares the Lord." What a promise! Do you believe it? See how your heart and mind are working right now as I ask you this simple question.

What are you hearing in your mind when you are posed this question? Do you believe that if you seek God with all your heart you will find Him? Notice the verse does not say you are to seek God with your mind. You are not to go to the beach at sunrise and stare off into the distance chanting. You do not have to go off into the wild and get back to nature risking your life by climbing a mountain or drowning in river rapids on some wild raft ride. The Bible says you are to seek God with your *entire* heart, and when you do that, you will find him. So I ask you now, are you ready to find God? Are you ready to discover the catalyst that will propel you into a transformation process leading you to a life of peace and contentment you thought only existed in fairy tales?

The most important choice you can ever make in your life is the choice to surrender to Jesus Christ as Lord of your life. The next most important choice you can make is to commit to learning and applying His Word in your life every day. To receive Jesus but to choose to walk inconsistently in and out of obedience guarantees you a life of strife, confusion, pain, sorrow, and sadness. Remember that old Sunday school lesson: obedience gets blessings, sin gets consequences. I take it you are reading this book because you already have made your choice for Jesus. That being the case, now is the time for you to choose to walk in the Spirit, to walk in obedience, and to walk in the abundance of a full, rich relationship with Him whom you have been seeking your entire life.

Part Three

The C4 Process

Chapter Eight

Breaking Free from a Life in the Flesh

"I have been driven many times to my knees by the overwhelming conviction that I had nowhere to go. My own wisdom, and that of all about me, seemed insufficient for the day." ~ Abraham Lincoln

C4 contains the essential elements necessary for you to finally break free of the yo-yo effect of sin in your life. While praying and asking forgiveness for your sins puts you in right standing with God, wouldn't it be better if you could just stop sinning all together. Do you believe it is possible to get beyond a cycle of sin and forgiveness in your life? The Bible says you are to be free from the power of sin in your life. Paul wrote to the Romans that they should not keep sinning so grace might abound. We need to stop sinning, begin walking in the Spirit, and enjoy not only the grace of forgiveness but the blessing of walking in the peace, joy, and contentment of life in the Spirit. Is it even possible for an authentic Christian to stop habitual sin? Paul answers this question in the letter to the Romans with an emphatic yes. When you understand that you are in Christ, and when you understand that you have a *new Christ* nature, you discover that you are no longer a slave to the Adam nature of sin but free to obedience *in Christ*. Then you will discover you have the power of the Holy Spirit to choose not to sin. No more addictions, no more excuses, no more blame shifting, no more blaming your parents, no more therapy, no more drugs to cope – simply free from the imputed and inherited nature of sin and free in imputed (meaning to relate to a particular cause) righteousness of the new nature *in Jesus Christ*. You get the righteousness of Christ by being in relationship with Him. He becomes the cause of our right living with Him.

The apostle Paul explained the dynamics of transforming from living a life dead in sin to living alive in Jesus Christ.

> And you, who once were alienated and enemies in your mind by wicked works, yet now He has reconciled in the body of His flesh through death, to present you holy, and blameless, and above reproach in His sight; if indeed you continue in the faith, grounded and steadfast, and are not moved away from the hope of the gospel which you heard, which was preached to every creature under

heaven, of which I, Paul, became a minister (Col. 1:21-23).

The word, *alienated* in the Greek language literally means to "transfer ownership" or to "be transferred to another owner." Being born into the race of Adam, we were born with the corruption of Adam's heart, mind, and with a dead spirit. God's remedy to the problem of our alienation is to reconcile us and redeem us back unto Himself through the cross of His son Jesus Christ.

With an understanding and daily practice of the C4 process, you will be set free from the things of this world. This daily practice of walking reconciled in the Spirit is what Paul meant when he said, "If indeed you continue in the faith, grounded and steadfast, and are not moved away from the hope of the gospel which you heard." You have to choose to walk in the mechanics of daily life choices, to continue in the faith, grounded, and steadfast. So here is the practical daily process you should use to continue in the faith: step one is *Convicting*, step two is *Convincing*, step three is *Compelling*, step four is *Conforming*. The critical path illustrated below is the sequence, in chain reaction, that is at the heart of your spiritual transformation.

An abundant life in Christ is comprised of understanding the cause and effect relationship of each of these fundamental transformation steps. There is no short cut to a spiritual life in Christ anymore than there is a short cut in farming or in a monarch butterfly going from crawling to flying. The rest of this book will take you through each step and explain how each functions in the life of an authentic Christian.

You will discover the cause and effect relationship that exists among each stage of the transformation process. It is similar to the way one domino falls into another domino starting a chain reaction of tipping dominos. So it is that all human beings choose their behavior based on what they think will happen to them. You follow the speed limit because you think if you don't you will be pulled over and receive a speeding ticket. You might speed because you do not believe you will get caught. You might experiment with drugs and sex because you do not believe that anything bad can happen if you try it just once. You choose to believe in Jesus Christ for salvation because you don't want to go to hell. You put off believing in Jesus Christ because you still want to sow some wild oats, and you believe you can accept Him as Savior tomorrow. Successful change, metamorphosis for anyone and especially for Christians, begins with having an accurate mental model, an accurate map of cause and effect. So let's begin the journey that will lead you to a victorious life in Christ.

CONVICTING – A CHANGE OF YOUR HEART

My expository teaching ministry focuses on helping people see what the Bible says, teaching them what the Bible means, and then encouraging them to take this spiritual wisdom and knowledge and *do* something with it to change their lives in

Jesus Christ. My professional work in organizational effectiveness and peak performance serves the same function – leading people to truth about who they are, how they behave, and how to live more productive, fruitful lives. Over the years I have discovered that of these three functions, applying the Word of God and living it out in changed behavior is the least practiced discipline of an authentic Christian. It is also the most frustrating aspect of watching smart people who know what do and have the capability to do it, behave so irrationally and destructively. Understand that you cannot apply to your life what you first do not know and believe. Sadly, there is a woeful lack of systematic Bible teaching, and so-called Christians are absolutely ignorant of the Word of God. Well now is the time to start closing this knowing and doing gap.

If the apostle Paul was right about anything in his teaching, it was certainly that spiritual understanding was to be evident in everyday practical and authentic Christian behavior. In Colossians 2:1 Paul writes that we have been raised with Christ. Notice that Paul writes in the past tense. We have *been raised* with Christ. This implies that first we died with Christ. In the words of the now dated saying, "born once, die twice – born twice, die once," we enter into the death of our flesh to be reborn in our spirit. Paul states that we have been raised with Christ, and if raised with Him, we should now be acting like Him.

What does acting like Christ look like, and how do I make this transformation? It all starts with what you choose to believe to be true in your heart.

The operative word is conviction – what you really believe to be true is what drives your thinking and behavior. Conviction is a work that begins in your heart. In Jeremiah 17:9, the Bible says, "The heart is deceitful above all things, and desperately wicked: who can know it?" We have a heart that was born in corruption and needs to be transplanted with an incorruptible heart of Jesus Christ. We need to accept what the Bible says as true about our hearts and the reason we need a heart transplant – out with the heart of Adam and in with the heart of Christ, begins our metamorphosis – our change of form from our inherited corruptible nature of Adam, to our reborn incorruptible nature in Christ.

Throughout his writing to the church at Colossae, Paul clearly introduces us to a process of spiritual transformation into the nature of the preeminent Christ. Using this letter as a guide, we will see what I am calling the C4 process imbedded in this instructional letter to those earlier believers. As I have stated before, unless you understand the process of spiritual transformation, you are very likely to be living a frustrated and defeated life in Christ. In the worst case, failing to understand the true gospel of the Bible, you will gravitate to false teaching and perversions of the gospel. Thinking that you are operating on sound doctrine, you will be building your house on the sanding land (Matt. 7:24-29). You must build your spiritual life on the solid rock of the true biblical doctrine of Jesus Christ, and that doctrinal truth is revealed through the systematic study of God's Word, the Holy Bible. Remember our little Irish mother who was sitting on a wealth of treasure and living like a pauper? Unless we know how this process works and how to apply it daily in our lives, we too are like this woman – in possession of great wealth but living in spiritual poverty.

C4, the process, begins with our salvation. Salvation occurs when we yield ourselves completely over to the Lord Jesus Christ – our reliance – trusting and clinging to the truth of the finished work of the cross of Calvary. We are being saved from ourselves and a life of rebellion against God. I have a strong sense that most Christians do not have a biblical understanding of salvation. I could be mistaken, but I believe, from my pastoral and teaching experiences, that most Christians do not really understand the destructive nature of sin and consequently, do not grasp the full importance of the death of Jesus Christ on the cross as a sacrifice for that sin. I could be wrong, and if I am, then someone needs to explain to me the reason so many Christians can have such a casual and cavalier attitude toward sin. If we fully comprehend and value the price of the forgiveness for our sin – the life of the very Son of God, Jesus Christ, then why do so many Christians continue to go on sinning as if it did not really matter?

Let's look for part of this answer by way of an analogy. Just imagine how a corrupt software program can infect a hard drive of a computer. The corruption can be undetectable to the user and working behind the scenes of the normal operating system yet still be causing errors in the output. So it is with the heart we inherited from the corrupted nature of Adam.

You might think that you can do nice things, like be kind and helpful – that you have a good heart. This is mere deception and delusion. In your Adam nature you are a sinner, and you sin because you have a sin nature. Pastor Chuck Smith, Calvary Chapel Costa Mesa, has a great way of teaching this fundamental principle. He always says that behavior reveals the heart of a person. So a man is not a horse thief because he steals a horse. He stole the horse because in his heart he was already a horse thief. You cannot leave any part of a defective software program on your computer and expect to get clean results in the output. So too, you cannot keep any part of your corrupt nature alive and expect to walk in the new life of the Spirit without that contamination causing havoc with your walk in the Spirit.

Let me try another analogy to convey the teaching point to you regarding your old nature and your new nature. In a hospital intensive care unit there can be two patients who are unconscious and connected to life support. Both patients look alive and have their vital signs responding on the monitors that indicate heart rate, blood pressure, and oxygen saturation levels. While they look identical in their physical appearance, one of these patients is really dead, brain dead with no viable brain function. Once the patient with no brain function is taken off life support, all vital body processes shut down and life ceases.

The problem for most Christians, especially new believers in Jesus Christ, is failing to recognize that their Adam nature must be taken off life support. The Adam nature has to be crucified with Christ so that the new nature can rise with a resurrected life in Christ. Rather than look at yourself as if your old nature could revive itself and come off life support, you need to account, reckon, and decide that your old nature is dead so you only function in your new nature in Jesus Christ.

The first thing we need to understand about sin is that it is our sin, and it originates in our corrupted heart, inherited from our flesh ancestor Adam. Accepting personal accountability and responsibility for your own sin opens the door for you to enter into the saving grace of God. Whether your sin is willful, in that you directly and intentionally violate the laws of God, or whether you sin accidently, out of ignorance, the result is the same – in your sin, you are falling short of the glory of God. In your sin, you are separated from God and at war with God. Just in case you really do not believe just how hideous and awful your sin is, God tells us that the wages of our sin is death. When you choose to sin you are in rebellion against God, rejecting Him, and choosing death (1Thess. 4:8).

So that is the reality of our sin. We are at war with God, and our very nature, the inherited sin nature of Adam, keeps us separated from God because in our sin we continually fall short of the glory of God. Adam was first created in the image of God. That image was a reflective image, like looking in a mirror, of the glory and holiness of the Godhead. Once Adam sinned, he corrupted that image and his very nature from the likeness of God to the likeness of sin and rebellion. You and I were born into this corrupted nature of Adam, and it is from this corrupted nature that we are set free when we confess our sin, submitting and surrendering ourselves to the Lordship of Jesus Christ.

By one historical fact, the act of obedience by Jesus Christ and His death on the cross, He became a substitute for our corruption and opened the door by the free gift of salvation for us to be transformed from a nature and life of corruption to His nature and life in the Spirit. Our transformation is a process of entering into the death of our flesh, our Adam nature, so we can be reborn and rise into a spiritual life in Jesus Christ. What a glorious promise and truth of the Holy Bible. Do you believe it?

Not only is our sin forgiven when we enter into this death to life process, but we also gain a legal standing, our justification in Jesus Christ. At one time we were at war with God and subject to His wrath. We are now at peace with God, justified and freed from the judgment of God. Beyond our right standing with God - our forgiveness and justification - the Bible says our sins are eradicated, ". . . having forgiven you all the trespasses. Having wiped out the handwriting of requirements that was against us . . . . He has taken it out of the way, having nailed it to the cross" (Col 2). I do not know exactly at what point in time you decided to stop being at war with God receiving the free gift of eternal life through the death and resurrection of Jesus Christ. I do know, however, that all of your sins went to the cross over two thousand years ago, and not only were they nailed with

Jesus to the cross but were wiped away as if they never existed.

One word describes the starting point for this spiritual transformation – conviction. There is a double meaning here, a play on words, if you will, that in our sin we stand convicted, sentenced to death. Then, when we come to a conscious awareness that we are dead in our sins, we receive conviction, the power of revealed truth that drives us to repentance and it is in repentance that we receive our salvation. Conviction, created from the revealed truth of Jesus Christ in our hearts, leads us to repentance. In this process of moving from conviction to repentance (the changing of our minds), we have to answer two fundamental questions. First, is it worth it? Is giving up a life of worldly power, possessions, pleasure, and pride worth a life of service to Jesus Christ? Second, can you do it? If it is not possible to be set free from the burden, the harm, the emptiness, the despair, and the tragedy of a life lived in serving self, then why try to do it? People do not give up behavior that gives them intense pleasure, even if self-destructive, just because they have a nice little chat with you on the four spiritual laws. The power of your own personal experience is necessary to compel someone to change. If your own life has no evidence of a life lived in the full glory of a resurrected life in Christ, then why would you expect anyone to come to Christ based on your witness?

Salvation is the outcome of a spiritual awakening that brings a change to my *heart*, which clears my *thinking*. My heart is then *compelled* by the Holy

Spirit to *conform* my corruptible nature into the incorruptible nature, image, and character of Jesus Christ. In the midst of this conviction, convincing, compelling, and conforming process, authentic Christians know exactly how to respond to temptation and the lure of the world, the flesh, and the devil. No longer a slave to sin and no longer choosing in the lust of my own desires to sin, I am free to walk in the power of the Holy Spirit, in righteousness. I put my old Adam nature to death as I pull the plug on life support and walk in the power and newness of life in Christ.

Recall that the real power of a transformed life in Christ is demonstrated in practical daily living. Things that we used to do in habits and behavior in the flesh nature of Adam, we simply should not be doing any more as an authentic Christian with a regenerated nature in Jesus Christ. No longer do I have to be trapped in a cycle of sin and forgiveness, living in the poverty level of my walk with the Spirit. Paul tells us in the letter to the Ephesians that we were dead in trespasses and sins meandering around to the dictates of the flesh, the world, and the devil. We had (note the past tense) a heart and spirit of disobedience. Yet God who is rich in His love and mercy even when we were dead in sin quickened our spirits, revived our spirits, and made us alive with Christ. Can you begin to grasp the truth of this fact? Can you understand and apply the C4 process in your life every day? *You are God's handiwork, workmanship, His poetry, and He is working to complete you and perfect you daily into the restored image of His Son.*

I am convinced that the reason many so-called Christians walk around defeated rather than living a fruitful, abundant, and victorious life in Christ is their failure to move productively through this C4 transformation process. We see that conviction is the start of any authentic Christian conversion experience. Conviction is something that happens in your heart. Your heart is the seat of your most deeply held beliefs – the seat of your core principles and values. What you believe to be true about anything drives your thinking, which ultimately frames your behavior, which creates the consequences of your life choices. Think back to what you have already read earlier in this book - what you choose to believe really matters. Unless Jesus Christ rules in our hearts, we never reach a point of transformation into His nature, character, and behavior. Paul wrote that if we confess with our mouths the Lord Jesus Christ and *believe* in our hearts that God raised Him from the dead, then we shall be saved (Romans 10:9). In this passage Paul is describing for us the mistake the Jews were making in seeking to use the law as a means to righteousness. Paul is showing them that the law confirms the corruptness of the Adam nature and the need for God's righteousness through His Son Jesus Christ. The Jews did not understand the purpose of the law, and as a result, Jesus became a stumbling to them and foolishness to the Gentiles.

Confession with the mouth begins with conviction in our hearts. This conviction is the heart felt belief that Jesus was raised from the dead, and with my mouth I confess this convicting truth unto salvation. We are saved by faith made by the confession of our mouths. Our confession is the tangible evidence that testifies to the grace of God and the change of my heart. My repentance, the changing of my mind from sin to obedience, sets me free from my Adam nature and begins my spiritual transformation into the nature of Jesus Christ.

Once again, the word, *believe*, means to cling to, to trust in, and to rely upon. You must surrender your entire being into the trust and the care of God. Without conviction in the heart there is no total surrender, and without total surrender there is no transformation process. You will live a frustrated life in only partial blessings and partial obedience as you vacillate back and forth from feeding your flesh while feebly attempting to walk in the Spirit. There is a metaphor that has made its way around office email for quite some time relating the story of two wolves that are fighting for dominance in the pack. The question in this valiant struggle is which wolf will win the fight? This metaphor applies to an authentic Christian who daily struggles between the flesh and spirit. Who wins in this fight? Well the answer is whichever one you feed the most. If you feed your flesh and starve your spirit, your flesh will win. If you starve your flesh and feed your spirit, your spirit will win. So where do we begin understanding how to starve our flesh and feed our spirit? Paul wrote, "Walk in the Spirit and you shall not fulfill the lusts of the flesh; for the flesh lusts against the Spirit, and the Spirit against the flesh (Gal. 5:16-17). The entire process starts with a heart of repentance, a change of your mind.

Part of the problem for many people is that we do not hear much about repentance in churches these days, at least not in most American churches. Repentance requires choice and personal responsibility, and you will not hear much about either one in American churches today. Yet without a heart of repentance you cannot begin to fully understand, develop, and live in the consistent and sustained walk of the Spirit.

You can most likely recall someone who received Jesus Christ as Lord and went on to serve Him with passion and consistent obedience. No doubt you saw major changes take place in the life of that person as they conformed to the nature and character of Jesus. I suspect you also know of a person who made the same claim to a profession of faith and had no life changes, no thought changes, and continued to walk in the life of the flesh. How can this be the case? Part of it has to do with the seed of the Word of God, the Word not taking root, the teaching of the Bible falling on a hard heart (see *The Parable of the Sower* in Mark 4:1-20, Matthew 13:1-23, and Luke 8:1-15). Ultimately it all boils down to what a person believes and chooses.

If you keep a hard heart, you will never begin your transformation process in a way that will complete you in the nature of Jesus Christ. So how about doing a little heart exam. Psalm 51:10 says, "Create in me a clean heart, O God: and renew a right spirit within me." David had committed terrible sins of betrayal, adultery, and murder. Yet as a man after God's own **heart**, he was broken in confession, repentance, and contrition. David demonstrated that he was not only really sorry (regret for his sin), he was painfully repentant, as he was greatly afraid that he had lost fellowship with God. That kind of belief, coupled with great fear in emotion, would compel most rational people to their knees. Can you pray that prayer? Can you ask God to create a clean heart in you? It is the only way to begin your transformation process on the solid Rock of Jesus Christ.

If you keep any part of your Adam heart alive, you risk not completing your transformation process. Don't you think it is time to let go of the things of this world and enter into the grace, peace, and rest your heavenly Father has prepared for you? The Bible tells us that Paul went out to preach on the Sabbath in Philippi, and a certain woman named Lydia heard the message (Acts 16:14). The Bible says the Lord opened her heart, and she acted on what she had heard in the words spoken by Paul. Immediately, both she and her entire household were baptized. Has the Lord opened your heart to what you have heard in this book? Take some time now to stop reading and to pray. Ask the Holy Spirit to open your heart and work this conviction deep into your heart. Pray for the eyes of your heart to be opened to the truth of God. To know God is to know the truth, and the Bible says the truth shall make you free. Take your time with this prayer and then continue to the next chapter to begin the work of renewing your mind.

Chapter Nine

Renewing Your Mind

And be not conformed to this world: but be ye transformed by the renewing of your mind, that ye may prove what is that good, and acceptable, and perfect, will of God. – Romans 12:2

CONVINCING – A CHANGE OF YOUR MIND

Once your heart has been secured in Christ, then we can move to the brain and the mind. So many people struggle in their walk with God because they try to start in the mind before the Spirit has begun to work in their hearts. This is why self-help, self-control, and behavior modification techniques eventually fail. You will never sustain a transformation experience unless your heart and mind are in alignment, operating in a synchronized manner. Pastor and leadership guru, John Maxwell, says it this way, "You see our belief determines our behavior. It's impossible ... for you and me to behave in a way that we don't believe." We have words to describe people who behave in contradiction to what they profess to believe. The word hypocrite comes to mind along with a host of mental illness terms. Suffice it for us to say, that unless we keep our hearts and minds aligned to consistent behavior, walking our talk as the cliché suggests, we will never have an abundant and productive life in the Spirit. Worse, as the subtitle of this book, "why Christians don't change" implies, we say we believe in Jesus, but we do not behave like we believe. Consequently, we are ineffective, disqualified if you will, to witness the gospel of Jesus Christ with credibility to a lost and desperate world.

The apostle John, writing in his first epistle, spells out this disconnect in far less gentle terms.

This is the message we have heard from him and declare to you: God is light; in him there is no darkness at all. If we claim to have fellowship with him yet walk in the darkness, we lie and do not live by the truth. But if we walk in the light, as he is in the light, we have fellowship with one another, and the blood of Jesus, his Son, purifies us from all sin. If we claim to be without sin, we deceive ourselves and the truth is not in us. If we confess our sins, he is faithful and just and will forgive us our sins and purify us from all unrighteousness. If we claim we have not sinned, we make him out to be a liar and his word has no place in our lives (1 John 1:5-10).

So you can clearly see from the Word that how we behave really reveals what we believe. Having an accurate understanding of how the human brain and mind function, including how the physical nature of the brain itself works will help us resolve this disconnect in the spiritual transformation of our lives in Jesus Christ.

The last chapter outlined our fundamental problem, namely, your outward behavior reflects the condition of your inner core – your heart. We were all born in the likeness of the first man Adam. That likeness is a corrupted nature and not the likeness of the original creation of man in the image of God. The remedy for this corrupted nature is a new nature in Jesus Christ. Writing to the Romans, Paul tells us that there is no condemnation to those who are in Christ Jesus. How is this possible? Paul tells us that there are two laws operating simultaneously. The first is the law of sin and death, and the other is the law of the Spirit of life in Jesus Christ (Romans 8). So as Adam was created incorruptible, holy in the image of God and became corrupted in sinful flesh, God sent his only begotten Son, Jesus, in the likeness of sinful flesh (Romans 8:3) that in His death and resurrection the corruptible becomes incorruptible again, and we are restored to a right relationship with our heavenly Father. Hence, the rightness of the law is fulfilled in us who now walk after the Spirit and not after the flesh.

It is absolutely imperative that you understand and fully comprehend what the Bible teaches about this transformation of your very nature. By faith, believing in the fact of the bodily death and resurrection of Jesus Christ, we obtain a new nature moving from corruptible flesh to incorruptible Spirit. This fact must be a fundamental truth in your heart. Otherwise, as Maxwell suggests, you can never behave in a way you do not believe. If you do not really believe in the fact that by grace through faith you are being transformed from a nature of death and sin into the nature of righteousness and holiness of Jesus Christ, you will not demonstrate behavior that consistently reflects what you claim to believe.

The battle for this belief takes places in your mind. The biggest barriers to change are found in our own minds, specifically, what we believe to be true about every aspect of our lives. We form mental maps or models in our beliefs that guide our behavior based on what we expect to get as a result. Unfortunately, many Christians live in a reactive mode to their immediate environment. They live life on autopilot failing to stop and think how an immediate reaction in choices reflects their core values, principle, ideals, and moral codes. As a result, they can end up in disastrous consequences, not because they purposed to choose bad things but merely because they failed to intentionally choose to do the right or better thing. The result is the same, however, as if they were not really choosing at all.

There are four possibilities for how the heart and the mind align: synchronizing in harmony of belief and thought, and ultimately manifesting in our accidental or intentional behavior.

	Heart of Adam	Heart of Christ
Mind of Christ	Heart of Adam/Mind of Christ *Religious Legalist*	Heart of Christ/Mind of Christ *Authentic Believer*
Mind of Adam	Heart of Adam/Mind of Adam *Self-Serving Sinner*	Heart of Christ/Mind of Adam *Carnal Believer*

There is only one possibility from the diagram above that ensures your salvation, your reconciliation, and your spiritual transformation and that is to have both the heart of Christ and the mind of Christ. Read and grasp the meaning of the words of the apostle Paul:

> For they that are after the flesh do mind the things of the flesh; but they that are after the Spirit, the things of the Spirit. For to be carnally minded is death; but to spiritually minded is life and peace. Because the carnal mind is enmity against God; for it is not subject to the law of God, neither in deed can it be. So then they that are in the flesh cannot please God (Romans 8:5-8).

Do you understand what the Bible is teaching you? You can only be at peace with God and please Him when you have both the heart and the mind of Christ. If you try to live in any other combination of your heart and mind, at worst, you risk your very salvation serving the law of sin and death. The other possibilities leave you frustrated in acts of self-righteousness and legalism on the one hand and then on the other, living as an unproductive and unfruitful Christian in a carnal mind with behavior that looks just like the unregenerate sinner. Let me give you an example of how this can play out in your life.

Back in the 1990s there was a revival of a popular phrase from the 19th century, "What would Jesus do?" Bracelets with the slogan "WWJD" became the popular fad of day. The intent was to cause a person to stop and think about life choices that would reflect walking in the steps of Jesus. If I can figure out what Jesus would do in a given situation, then the logic suggests that is what I should do too. The main biblical problem with this thinking has to do with the origination of the "WWJD" idea. Writing in 1896, Charles Sheldon had a theology shaped on Christian Socialism that he placed in his fictional novel, *In His Steps*. His purpose driven interpretation of Christianity was in social causes. Jesus is a social redeemer, not Lord and Savior. To really know and discover what Jesus *would do*, we are better served in discovering from the Bible what Jesus *believed*, especially about Himself, and not from following the thinking of a fictional account for how one might make moral choices.

You can only be assured of your eternal destiny by abiding in the heart of Christ and the mind of Christ living a life conformed to the nature of Jesus. What a tragedy for so many people today who are trusting in something other than the full Gospel of the Holy Bible and who may be heading to their ultimate destruction. "But ye are not of the flesh, but in the Spirit, if so it is that the Spirit of God dwells in you. Now if any man has not the Spirit of Christ, he is none of his." While this statement is tragic, there is good news for those who believe.

With Christ dwelling in your heart and your mind, you have been raised up with Jesus from a life of sin and death. We no longer owe a debt to sin to live after the flesh. If you live after the flesh, the Bible says you will surely die. Whether you have the flesh heart of Adam or the flesh mind of Adam, or both, the Bible says, "if you live after the flesh you will surely die but if after the Spirit you shall live" (Romans 8:13). Believe me when I tell you that the key to finding abundance in Jesus Christ is to renew your mind, taking on God's thoughts and turning those thoughts into beliefs that you build upon as your core foundation in your heart. What you choose to believe becomes what you think and ultimately comes out in your behavior. Consider that following example to prove my point.

Vinson Filyaw waited for the school bus to depart from its rural stop in a wooded area of Elgin, South Carolina. He had been watching his target for days – a 14 year old walking up the secluded driveway all alone. Here is how he told the story to authorities in his confession written from his prison cell. "I remembered seeing one of the girls from the high school bus go up a wooded driveway. That is when I started thinking. If I could make my way through the woods to her house, I could abduct her from there."

Posing as a police officer with a homemade patch on his shirt, Vinson Filyaw approached his young victim as she turned up the drive way. He told her she was under arrest as he handcuffed her and led her away to an underground bunker he had dug in the woods. Nearly two weeks later she was rescued by police, and Filyaw was arrested. "I began thinking how I could do it," he wrote. How we choose to behave is always a product of what we believe and how we think. What a powerful example of how a person can believe "it" in his heart, conceive "it" in his mind, and then carry out those thoughts in his behavior.

When our lives are not what we want them to be, you can be certain that you have a hidden belief in your heart to something other than what you say you believe. If you say you hate sin but you continue to enjoy the pleasure of it, the apostle John says you are lying to yourself and to God. You cannot "fake it to make it." These hidden desires are responsible for the discrepancy and for the inconsistency that is evident between what you profess to believe and how you actually behave.

So how do I get my behavior to align with the heart and mind of Christ? The answer is you choose to do it. You decide to do it. You resolve to do it. You commit to do it. You get in accountability with another believer, and you partner together to do it. You get in the Word of God, and you let the *dunamis* of the Word and the dynamic power*s* of the Holy Spirit *compel* you to do it. You walk in the Spirit and stay immersed in the things of the Spirit. You take your flesh off life support, bury it, and walk in the resurrected, metamorphosis of your new life in Jesus Christ.

Paul, in a similar teaching to the Colossians, exhorted them to believe that since they had **been raised** with Christ, they were to seek those things which are above in heaven and to set their desires and affections on the things above. Paul tells them *they* must decide to choose where to put their hearts and minds. Then Paul tells them specifically the behaviors that will follow from this alignment of heart and mind. Paul is taking for granted that these believers have their hearts and minds in alignment with Christ; and therefore, their behavior will naturally follow as a result of the transformation that has taken place in their desires, affections, and thinking. So how do I keep my mind on the things above, and how do I renew my mind daily? I am glad you asked.

Sometimes Christians are reluctant to let go of their problems and self-destructive behaviors because they feel special, unique, and enjoy the attention they get from others by staying in their problems. Their problems become how they identify themselves –

like the lame man at the pool of Bethesda. Remember Jesus asked him very dramatically, "Do you want to be healed?" Certain people love to be victims of the consequences of their choices. They seek out ways to confirm their beliefs that they are hopeless. They insist on *believing* that their circumstances are beyond the miracle working power of God. They demand that we continue to feel sorry for them. Sadly, they resist being taught that in reality they are living in self-limiting and self-imposed behaviors framed from their faulty thinking and false beliefs. Sadly, as the apostle John would say, they choose to live in their lies either consciously or unconsciously.

Change comes as a matter of choice. You renew your mind and begin to think differently because you choose to do so. Change is not about what you *feel* like doing. Before you decide to choose anything about your behavior, what Paul calls "putting on the new nature" in his letter to the Colossians, you have to want to change. This book is designed to be a guide for your behavior. It is a guide to help you live an abundant and highly productive life in Jesus Christ. My sense is there are a lot of people who want to have the blessings of being in Christ without being willing to change their behavior to receive those blessings. If you can think differently, and I know you can, you can change your life. The truth is that most of your habitual problems, which are related to failing to behave like Jesus, are the manifestation of living in the same bad thinking, practicing the same bad habits, and believing the lie that you cannot change.

How willing are you to change? Do you have the desire to change? Convincing others to see themselves differently, choosing differently, thinking differently, and behaving differently is not easy. I am asking you to trust me on this point. I have dedicated my life to teaching and influencing people to change their hearts, minds, and behavior. Not only are some people skeptical about change, some actively resist change while they hold onto lies and irrational, crazy behaviors and beliefs. You will never change anything about your fleshly desires and affections until you want to change. Wanting to change and desiring to change come with a new way of thinking and the daily renewing of your mind.

RENEWING YOUR MIND

There is much we can learn from medical research that tells us how the flesh brain and the flesh mind work. The Bible tells us how the Spirit mind works. The problem for many Christians who struggle to change their fleshly behavior, namely, anger, wrath, malice, sexual lusts, covetous, idolatry, pleasure, power, and possessions is that they do not want to change. Simply put, far too many people who claim to be Christians still like the pleasures of sin even while knowing that participating in these pleasures will lead them to a life of pain, sorrow, and suffering. Just imagine, here you are living on death row in prison. You received a pardon. The door of your prison cell is set open. You are free to go. You do not believe that you are free because you know you deserve to die. Worse, you have grown so accustomed to living on death row that rather than leave to discover life in the freedom from the cell, you choose to live on death row and forfeit the benefits of freedom. Instead of walking out of your open prison cell, you continue to live on death row and die in your death row cell. What a tragedy, but this is exactly how I see far too many Christians living their lives all because they choose to live in self-defeating thinking and behavior.

People are not about to give up living a life of pleasure in sin and the world simply by verbal persuasion. The power of their mental maps is a stronghold holding them back. When my children were younger, I wanted them to see the consequences of a life given over to the world, the flesh, and the devil, so I took them on field trips. Traveling with my military job, I had to go to Philadelphia, so I took the family with me. What better way for them to learn about our nation's history than from direct, personal experience in the city that founded the birth of our nation? We traveled all over the historic sites of the city to include a visit to the tomb of Benjamin Franklin.

If you have never been to Philadelphia, the cemetery with Franklin's tomb is not in the best part of town. The grave of Benjamin Franklin and his wife, Deborah, lay beside the grave of their daughter and her husband at Christ Church Cemetery. Franklin said, *"A penny saved is a penny earned,"* yet the tradition practiced by throngs of visitors is to throw pennies on his grave. Various sources suggest the discarded pennies amount to about $6,000 each year, which is donated to the poor – and unfortunately, the poor, the homeless, the alcoholics, and other "people of the street" abound in this part of the city.

As we made our way to the entrance of the cemetery, we literally had to step over a man who was unconscious and laying in his own human waste and vomit; obviously a street dweller or homeless man. The smell was horrendous, and people moved about and around him oblivious to his existence. We literally had to lift our small daughter over the man to gain access to the cemetery. Our children learned a powerful lesson in life choices that day – the consequences and the quality of your life today are determined by your thinking and choices you made yesterday, a year ago, and five years ago.

Mental strong holds are predominately related to false concepts and beliefs that you store in your brain as memory of past events. There is a ton of medical research on brain function that validates how the brain actually works to store and recall memory. The sources are far too many for me to list here, so I have included them in an exhaustive list at the end of the book. The process of renewing your mind begins with you understanding your need to take an active role and participate with the power of the Holy Spirit so your thinking can change.

When Jesus told the lame man at the pool of Bethesda to get up and walk, Jesus did not levitate the man. The man had to get up on his own. He had to participate in the power of the healing that Jesus was extending to him. Likewise, you have to participate in the healing of your flesh mind: the transformation in your mind of Adam to the mind of Christ. You have to develop mental toughness. Mental toughness is the ability, the acquired habit of staying motivated and focused on the things of the Spirit in the midst of temptations, distractions, difficult life circumstances, and sometimes just the sheer, mundane routines of every day life. The act of renewing your mind is you taking active, intentional effort every day to reconnect to your core nature in Jesus, your core beliefs in the Word of God, and your fundamental desire to live your life pleasing to God.

Renewing your mind is also about learning to think more clearly and more effectively. When you find yourself making a choice for sin that is in direct conflict with the desire to please God, you must discover the underlying root cause. Every time you confront an old habit of your flesh with your new awareness of sin in the Spirit, you will discover an area of your life that still seeks control over you. The life you are living right now was created, in part, based on your ability to think clearly and effectively. Many writers have stated before me that success in life and at work is the byproduct, the direct result, of your ability to think well. So too is your walk with Jesus. You must learn to think clearly and effectively, manage your emotions, subdue your impulses, yield to the power of the Holy Spirit, and hide God's word in your heart so that you choose not to sin against Him.

Many frustrated Christians are living in self-defeating habits because they are choosing to live in self-limiting thinking habits. Self-centered, negative, impulsive, and just plain lazy thinking can lead people to all kinds of ineffective and harmful life choices. Unfortunately, we have far too many examples to prove this last statement true. Dare I mention the names of prominent religious and political figures whose lives have been devastated by willfully choosing to cave to sexual lust? What could they have possibly been thinking, we ask, when they put their reputations and their families in such grave jeopardy for a moment of lustful passion? The answer, sadly enough, is that they could not have been thinking, at least not thinking effectively. The internal struggle of their fleshly drives and desires were stronger than their ability to act in a morally responsible way. Unless you have been crucified with Christ, these unresolved desires of your flesh will lead you into repetitive self-sabotaging behaviors. As a result, you too will continue to quench the Holy Spirit's power in your transformation process and feel powerless and hopeless in living an abundant life in Christ.

Renewing of your mind is the daily process of keeping your heart in alignment with your commitment to surrender your life as a servant to the Lord Jesus Christ and allowing this commitment to influence you in how you choose to see your current situations, yourself and others. It is a daily habit of asking, "search my heart O' God." When you were born again, you made the conscious effort to surrender your entire life over to Jesus Christ. That means giving Jesus complete control over your body, heart, mind, will, and emotions. This means everything you think about doing, or desire to do, you must first ask Jesus for permission. Do you want to go back to the old bar and have a few drinks with old, worldly friends? You have to ask Jesus permission. You want to go back to those old pornography sites on the Internet? You have to ask Jesus permission. You want to gossip, steal, lie, and cheat? You want to "super size" that greasy burger and fries to console your flesh's unhealthy eating habits? You want to go on that shopping spree to comfort your flesh? As an authentic Christian, you have to ask Jesus permission.

The great news is that as you begin to study the Word of God, hide it in your heart, seek to please God, and live in the power of the Holy Spirit, then you will no longer have the desire to satisfy your flesh. You will develop the desire to live your life to bring pleasure to God. You will discover as you renew your mind daily in the things of God and begin walking with the Holy Spirit, you have been set free from the things of this world. This is where mental toughness comes into play. You cannot be lazy and complacent in the work and effort you are required to do to renew your mind. Jesus told the lame man at the pool of Bethesda, get up, take up your bed, and walk. The Bible tells us that the man obeyed Jesus, and he was immediately made well. Now it is your turn. Are you ready to be made well? You are on your way when you learn how to intentionally choose to walk in the Spirit and apply the chain reaction process of C4 to your daily life. Are you ready to be healed?

Chapter Ten

The Holy Spirit in the Life of a Believer

He said to them, "Did you receive the Holy Spirit when you became believers?" They answered him, "We have never even heard that there is a Holy Spirit." And when Paul laid (his) hands on them, the Holy Spirit came upon them, and they spoke in tongues and prophesied. – Acts 19:2,6

This book is about teaching you how to live a victorious and abundant life in Jesus Christ. We spent a great deal of time in the beginning talking about the power of choosing, personal responsibility, and aligning what we believe to be true with the consequences of our behavior. You make a conscious choice to act always predicated on what you believe to be true. The problem is that we are capable of being deceived into believing something to be true even if it is a lie. So the real key is making sure that what we believe to be true really is the truth.

This is the reason we keep going back to the Word of God. You can believe the Bible to be the source of all truth. When you build your mind on values, principles, and beliefs, it is essential that you do so based on the Word of God. The problem for so many Christians is that they spend more time filling their hearts and minds with the world instead of the Word. My personal experience, when I hear someone say something they believe to be true, is to ask them why and on what evidence they base their belief. It has always been the case, particularly something relating to God and the Bible, that the person has read some fringe, on the edge, book. As my mentor, Pastor Chuck Smith has said, "When you hear something that is way off the wall, you can bet the person did not get it from the Bible."

We live in the fundamental reality that our flesh nature and the Holy Spirit are at war with each other (Gal. 5:17). This concept is a fundamental belief that you must accept as absolute truth. Any time we try to make peace with or simply surrender ourselves back to the flesh, we will end up in spiritual pain and suffering. Once we lose the emotional hurt of the experience, Satan comes back with another round of deception to lure us back into the same behavior over and over again. It is terribly painful to make an outward commitment to follow Jesus and then make choices that are in direct opposition to fulfilling that commitment.

You must begin to believe that God wants you to have victory in your life and victory over your flesh. He wants this for us so much that He has provided the way to our victorious living – providing us the opportunity to be in Jesus Christ and to walk and live our lives in harmony with the power of the Holy Spirit.

> But you shall receive power when the Holy Spirit has come upon you; and you shall be witnesses to Me in Jerusalem, and in all Judea and Samaria, and to the end of the earth (Acts 1:8).

We receive the "dynamic" power of God that enables us to walk free from sin and live a victorious and abundant life in Jesus Christ. Once you get your heart and mind aligned in agreement with the truth of God's Word, you release the power of the Holy Spirit in your life to compel you to the conforming nature and behavior of Jesus. There are two things that can get in the way of you being successful in applying the C4 process: your intellect and your emotions. The only access Satan has into your Holy Spirit empowered life is in your mind. He will try to confuse your thinking; the intellectual part of your mind, and he will try to control you by triggering negative emotions like fear and discouragement. Discouragement has tremendous power over the lives of people. Literally, the word *discouragement* means to "take away the strength of the heart." I like to interpret it as the attempt by someone to "put your heart out of business." The Bible tells us (Eph 6: 16-18) to put on the shield of faith and the helmet of salvation as a way of guarding our minds against the attacks of the devil.

In ancient warfare the shield was essential to warding off the first round of battle, the hail of fiery arrows. Commanders would commence a battle with an archery assault. The intent of this constant barrage of arrows was to demoralize the opposing force and compel them to break ranks, to weaken their resolve. In the ancient Battle of Thermopylae between the Persians and the Greeks, Persian King Xerxes bragged that his arrows would blot out the sun. Spartan King Leonidas did not lose heart and is recorded to have returned a reply to Xerxes stating, "Then we shall fight in the shade." When Satan comes to discourage us with his fiery arrows, we too need to stand with the shield of faith and fight the good fight and not lose heart. The power of the Holy Spirit will keep your heart in business.

We also need to protect our heads with the helmet of salvation. Fear and discouragement work in both the heart and the mind. Fear is an emotional reaction to a belief. I believe that God is asking me to do something I do not believe I can do. I believe that if I try, I will fail. I believe that God does not really love me. Faulty thinking can lead to negative emotions that lead to behaviors that are counterproductive to walking in the Spirit and living a victorious life in Christ. The interesting thing is that we get to choose what we believe. The reason intelligent people are capable of behaving in so many self-defeating and self-destructive habits is simply a matter of what they choose to believe to be true. If you say you love God and you believe God loves you and wants the very best for your life, why in heaven's name would you choose to behave in a way that would assure you of being robbed of your desired results?

The answer I get from most people when I ask them this question is - "I can't help it," or "I'm bipolar," or "I am an addict," or something else that indicates that these people do not believe they are making free choices to cooperate with Satan and participate in flawed thinking and life choices that will lead to their destruction. They start with a belief that says I am not responsible, or I am not capable, which suggests that they are victims and cannot be held personally accountable for their choices, actions, and behaviors. Well I have good news for you if your life fits this description. The dynamic power of God that filled an upper room in Jerusalem nearly 2000 years ago is the same power that is available to you today, tomorrow, and the rest of your life. The shield of faith, believing all that the Bible says is true, and the helmet of salvation, God's remedy for discouragement and other negative emotions are still at work to defeat the scheming treachery of the devil. The dynamic power of God will set you free from faulty thinking and negative emotions. All you need to do is believe that fact to be true.

When you find yourself caving in to a desire of your flesh, you have to ask yourself, "What do

I really believe, and what am I committed to at this moment?" My guess is that if you will ask yourself these questions, you will discover that you still have the desire to enjoy some pleasure of the world whether physical, emotional, or material in nature. You will discover that there is still a part of your Adam nature that you enjoy and that you have not yet crucified with Christ.

To begin your journey to freedom, you must be honest enough to tell yourself the truth about what you really lust after in the so-called pleasures of the world. You must accept responsibility for this lust, stop pretending to be a victim and blame shifting, and realize that you are still choosing to hold onto these ungodly desires. By exposing what is really in your heart that is driving your choices, you will be able to confess your sin, begin to change your mind (repentance), and begin to live your abundant life in Christ.

QUENCHING THE SPIRIT

Remember that change can be difficult even when we desire it. Learning how to yield your heart and mind to the power of the Holy Spirit may not come easy when you have had daily practice at doing your own thing for twenty, thirty, or more years. The key is that once you learn to surrender, things will not be as hard. Ignoring your hidden fleshly desires may delay the pain of dealing with past choices but guarantees that you will continue down a repetitive pattern of the cycle of sin and forgiveness, keeping you from living your abundant life in Christ.

As a teenager, my wife worked as a lifeguard at a local swimming club near her home. She has shared with me the fundamentals of life guard training from time to time. The one thing I remember her telling me is that you never swim all the way to the drowning person if they are still struggling in the water. In their panic to survive, the potential victim can drown themselves and the lifeguard. The rescue swimmer is trained to swim near the struggling victim and wait for them to exhaust themselves and then move in to begin the rescue hold and guide them back to safety.

This swimming example can serve as a metaphor in our lives with Jesus Christ. We can quench the power of the Holy Spirit trying to save ourselves or do it "my way," as the old Frank Sinatra song sadly suggests. We can flail away screaming for help, but it is not until we surrender ourselves totally in mind and body that the power of the Holy Spirit can become operational in our lives. When we continually make choices that contradict what we say we believe and what we say we desire, it is imperative that we expose the lie that exists in our heart and mind. We must expose that carnal part of our nature that has yet to die in Christ. By exposing the darkness of these hidden beliefs, we gain the freedom to stand and walk in the light of the truth of God's Word.

The apostle Paul addressed aspects of carnal Christianity in his writings to the Corinthinians and the Colossians. In describing the behavior of the natural man and the spiritual man, Paul provides us with a description of the carnal man. This is a person who claims to have the heart of Christ –claims to have received Jesus as their Savior but has not come to the place where they have crucified themselves with Jesus. From our previous example, these are the people with the heart of Christ and the mind of Adam and consequently, the flesh is still ruling in their lives. Jesus is Savior, as you have heard people say. Jesus has not become the Lord of their lives. In such a situation, there is no power of the Holy Spirit operating in their lives either.

If you really want to change your life, you must learn to make new choices, better choices, and more effective choices. C4 gives you a practical tool to apply in your daily life to stay connected to the power of the Holy Spirit. When you walk in the Spirit, you will discover the power necessary to break free from your life in the flesh and experience a real change of direction in your life. Every time you make a new and godly choice, you will experience the increasing power of the Holy Spirit and this power will keep you from drifting away from the solid foundation, the Rock, Jesus Christ.

Living in Hawaii on a military assignment, the entire family enjoyed our weekly beach activities. Our children were the perfect age at 14, 12, and 10 to enjoy boogie boarding and body surfing. They were also at the perfect age to be free from the natural sense of risk and danger. We preceded each trip to the beach with a safety briefing, in good military fashion of course. We would identify our rally point on the beach and mark it with our cooler, towels, and identification marker. If you have never experienced the surf on the north shore of Oahu, then you do not know the danger of drifting in the pull of the current when you are in the water. We always cautioned our children to stay aligned with our beach marker. As you might imagine with young teenagers, it was only a matter of time before mom was running down the beach yelling at them to move back up the shoreline. Inevitably, they would drift off course because of their inattentiveness while having so much fun in the pleasure of the surf.

We can also drift in our walk with the Holy Spirit if we do not have our feet firmly planted on the Rock, Jesus Christ. He never moves; we do. He never falters; we do. He never fails; we do. The Bible promises us that He is the same yesterday, today, and forever. We must remain committed to keeping our eyes focused on Jesus and making sure we are not drifting in lazy or inattentive thinking. The key is to stay focused by reading the Word daily, praying daily, staying in fellowship, and choosing to walk in obedience to the Word of God. Each time you stop, think clearly, and choose to act in the character of Jesus Christ, you propel yourself farther into your metamorphosis journey conforming to His nature. As you do, you free yourself to walk consistently, with great confidence, with meaning, purpose, and the heavenly value your Father has created for you.

Chapter Eleven

Conformed to His Image

For whom he did foreknow, he also did predesti-
nate to be conformed to the image of his Son, that
he might be the firstborn among many brethren.
Romans 8:29

Chapter eight of the Apostle Paul's letter to the Romans is a wonderful description of how our new and wonderful life has transformed into the nature and character of Jesus Christ. In this chapter, we discover God the Father's everlasting love for us and the key elements of living the Spirit-filled life. The Spirit intercedes for us. The Spirit leads and guides us. The Spirit empowers us, and it is by the Spirit's indwelling presence within us that we are conformed to the nature of Jesus Christ.

I regret that the ancient scholars who divided the Bible into chapters and verses decided to separate the end of chapter seven from the beginning of chapter eight. The victory for our lives is found in Jesus Christ. The apostle Paul writes of his wretchedness through the main section of chapter seven. He refers to himself some forty times between verses thirteen and twenty-four. I have found it to be the case that we tend to become totally self-absorbed when we begin to recognize our wretchedness. Our struggle with sin becomes personal. It is our struggle, our fight, and we want to take the credit and the glory for overcoming sin in our lives. The problem is that it is impossible for us to save ourselves. Paul's declaration of his wretchedness is not so much a confession of his sinful nature as it is an admission of the impossibility to please God in his own works, his own efforts, and his own attempt at keeping the Law. Paul's cry, "O wretched man that I am," is a cry of despair and futility. Ultimately, it is a cry of surrender.

"Who will deliver me from this body of death?" Again Paul makes an illusion to the apt description of being chained to a rotting corpse. You recall from an earlier chapter that the practice of being strapped to a dead body is a form of punishment. Here Paul makes reference to his own feelings of absolute despair in regards to coexisting with his own corrupt and rotting flesh. "Who will deliver me?" he cries. Paul discovers that answer by taking the focus off his current circumstances and looking at himself from the balcony while playing the lead role on stage. Paul is asking himself a rhetorical question because he already knows who is delivering him from his wretched state of despair. The freedom Paul is looking for lies in the reality of Jesus Christ. As soon as Paul recognizes that his freedom is not dependent upon his own efforts, he begins to give thanks. I strongly believe that one of the main strong holds blocking the power of the Spirit in the lives of many people is an ungrateful and unthankful heart. Not our dear brother Paul. He declares, "I thank God."

Like Paul, some of you are looking in the wrong places for your deliverance and the healing of your wounded soul. Some people turn to psychology and to hundreds of self-help books and feel good gurus. Others turn to psychiatrists and drugs to numb the pain of the internal stress they experience when they struggle in their beliefs and behavior; hence, what they believe and how they behave are in direct conflict with how an authentic Christian should believe and behave. Still others turn to life coaches, teachers, and motivational speakers when all they need to answer the deepest pain of their heart is a Savior. Your answer and your victory are waiting for you in Jesus Christ.

In transition to chapter eight, Paul tells us, "There is therefore now no condemnation to those who are in Christ Jesus, who do not walk according to the flesh, but according to the Spirit." The logic of Paul is clear in this passage. In fact, at one point in time, I am told, Stanford Law School students were required to study the Roman letter not for its spiritual content but for the construct of its logical reasoning. Paul is constructing a logical argument that since God the

Father has no condemnation for His Son, neither does He have any condemnation for those who are *in* His Son. God is in us through the Holy Spirit, and we are in God by our faith. Paul is crystal clear here; if we are one in Jesus Christ, we have no condemnation. Consider the alternative. If you are not in Jesus Christ, then you are in condemnation. This is why the Bible message is hated throughout the world. Jesus is the only way to be reconciled to the Father. There is no condemnation *only* for those who are in Christ Jesus. Paul now has peace for his wretched heart – he is at one with his Savior. You too can find this peace as you conform to the nature, character, and behavior of Jesus Christ.

The good news of Romans chapter eight is that we are free. We are free from the corrupting influence of our flesh. We are free from self-righteousness and hypocrisy. We are free from the worldly love of self. We are free from the power of sin in our lives. Finally, we are free from guilt, and perhaps most importantly, we are free from death. Sin was condemned in the death of Jesus, so the condemnation of our sin was nailed to the cross. God now wants the Holy Spirit to rule over our lives and for us to live in obedience by our desire to please and serve Him. When you allow the flesh to usurp position of authority over the Spirit, you will live in turmoil and find yourself recycling into patterns of sin we discussed in the last chapter. We recognize the existence of the flesh, but we live in the reality and understanding that the flesh has no power over us. We now walk in the power of the Spirit, and we pattern our lives conformed into the image of our Savior.

When you are born again, you not only receive the free gift of eternal life in Christ Jesus, you also receive the Holy Spirit who has power over the flesh.

> But you are not in the flesh but in the Spirit, if indeed the Spirit of God dwells in you. Now if anyone does not have the Spirit of Christ, he is not His. And if Christ *is* in you, the body *is* dead because of sin, but the Spirit *is* life because of righteousness. But if the Spirit of Him who raised Jesus from the dead dwells in you, He who raised Christ from the dead will also give life to your mortal bodies through His Spirit who dwells in you (Romans 8:9-11).

Confusion about the role of the Holy Spirit in the life of a believer is in many ways responsible for Christians living in a Romans chapter seven Christian life. From a biblical perspective, there is no such thing as a non-spirit filled believer. When you choose to believe in the Lord Jesus Christ for salvation, you receive the Holy Spirit. Whether or not you walk in the power of the Spirit or have the power of the Spirit released in your life is a different matter.

There are three distinct events regarding the working of the Holy Spirit in an authentic Christian. These events are designated in three Greek prepositions: *para, en*, and *epi*. Firstly, there is the *para* experience where you have the Holy Spirit *with* you. This is the relationship we have with the Holy Spirit prior to our conversion and acceptance of Jesus Christ. The purpose of the Holy Spirit being with us is to draw us to salvation. Secondly, we have the *en* experience of the Holy Spirit. Once we commit our lives to Christ we receive the Holy Spirit *in* us. Authentic Christians receive the *pneuma*, the literal presence of the breath of God's spirit inside them as a byproduct of the conversion experience. By the indwelling power of the Spirit we begin our transformation into the nature and character of Christ. Thirdly, the Holy Spirit releases power to us for ministry. The *dunamis*, the dynamic power of the Holy Spirit *comes upon* me, *comes over* me, and *overflows* from me in acts of service and ministry for the cause of Christ. All authentic Christians are Spirit filled. Sadly, not all Christians have the power of the Spirit pouring forth from their lives in acts of service and ministry. To claim to be a Christian without believing in the indwelling and over flowing power of the Holy Spirit in your life, is to live in the wretchedness that Paul confessed in Romans chapter seven.

Paul is describing at the end of chapter seven the wretched state of trying to keep the Law and live in righteousness by his own efforts. We can never attain a level of excellence in our pursuit of the nature of Jesus with the effort of the flesh. The wretchedness Paul so dramatically declares about himself is this futile cycle of effort and failure. In utter desperation Paul cries out, "Who shall deliver me from this body of death?" We find the answer in, "I thank God through Jesus Christ our Lord." Only by being in Jesus do we find the desire and the means to walk in the Spirit and conform to the image of the Son.

We enter into oneness with Jesus Christ by identifying with His death and resurrection. Doing so, we now have the Holy Spirit's power to overcome the flesh. We also have the Holy Spirit to lead us, to guide us, and to intercede for us before the Father. It is because of this dynamic relationship that Paul can now proclaim the transition that is described in chapter eight, "There is therefore now no condemnation to them who are in Christ Jesus who walk not after the flesh, but after the Spirit." We are in Christ Jesus, and since God the Father does not condemn Jesus, He does not condemn us. Now here is the final connection to C4. The purpose of God is revealed through the entire process of conviction, convincing, and compelling in which we would be conformed into the image of Jesus Christ. Born after the image of Adam, we are regenerated into and reborn into the image of God by conforming to the nature of Jesus. Who does this work? God Himself as we learn in Romans 8:29, "For whom he did foreknow, he also did predestinate to be conformed to the image of his Son, that he might be the firstborn among many brethren."

What a wonderful promise from our heavenly Father. His desire is for us to regenerate in a second birth with the goal of us being conformed to the image of his Son. Once you become aware that the primary goal of our salvation is to be restored to the original creation of God, the C4 process becomes evident throughout all of the scriptures. In Genesis 1:26, God said, "Let us make man in our image." God told Adam and Eve to be fruitful and multiply. I find it interesting that Adam and Eve did not have any children until after they were expelled from the Garden of Eden. We are descendents of Adam and Eve in their fallen state. In Genesis 5, we see that Adam was made in the likeness of God. Now when Adam reproduces, he does so in his own image and not in the image of God. Since Adam's nature was corrupted by his sin, everything created in his image has been corrupted. There is no amount of self-help available to restore us into the image of the Son in our corrupted nature. Hence, Paul's futile acknowledgement, "What a wretched man I am."

Wretched we once were in the nature of Adam, but now in Christ we have been redeemed and are being transformed and conformed into the image of the Son. This process of moving from conviction: the work of God in our hearts, and the convincing: the work He does in our minds, releases the compelling power of the Spirit to complete this transformation miracle in our lives conformed into the image of the Son. Jesus spoke of this process as well in his final moments with the disciples just prior to the crucifixion.

In John 14-15, we see Jesus preparing the disciples for His death, resurrection, and ultimately, His ascension into heaven. Do not let your hearts be troubled. I am surrounded on a daily basis with people who have troubled hearts. So many people are trying to live up to self-imposed expectations of others as they their lives. This is a trap of Satan to keep you mentally, emotionally, and physically fatigued. When you live your life to fulfill the expectations of others, you miss out on living the life God intended for you. Do not let your hearts be troubled. When you live with a troubled heart, it is very difficult to live in the grace and peace of God. When you are not living in peace, it is very hard to produce the fruit of the Spirit in your life. Joy and peace are supposed to be evident in the life of a person who claims to believe in God. Without joy and peace in our lives, it is very difficult to live a productive life as a Christian. Our own lives must reflect to others around us that living in Jesus makes a difference in how one chooses to live in this world and prepares for eternity.

Even for those of us who serve in formal ministry capacities, we have to be careful that we do not project a view that life as a Christian is hard, or that ministry is a burden. We should never sound like we are whining and complaining about surrendering our lives to Christ. What we project to others from our own lives in Christ is our witness. Being at peace with God ought to be reflected in our character and behavior. Simply stated, we ought to act as if we really trust God to be and do all the Bible tells us. Ultimately, it is in how we live our lives in front of those who are still lost in sin, as to whether they will give any ear to what they hear us say about the gospel. Someone recently told me that as Christians we need to be very attentive to how we live our lives. We may be the only Bible anyone ever reads. What a powerful thought. As we claim to be in Christ, we are supposed to be bearing fruit. Our lives are supposed to be making a difference for the Gospel of Jesus Christ. Have you examined the quality of your fruit lately?

A FINAL WORD

I made you a promise in the beginning of this book that I was going to teach you how to close the gap between what you say you believe to be true about being a Christian and how you actually behave as a Christian. The C4 process is a tool you can use to align what you say you believe with how you actually behave. Everything starts with knowing what the Bible says to be true. This may require some hard work on your part in adjusting your thinking regarding the traditions of your past. Many things that churches teach, while part of the religious tradition of that church and denomination, are not explicit teachings found in the Holy Bible. If we truly want to walk in the Spirit and enjoy the abundant life in Christ we are promised, we must commit to not only knowing what the Bible says, but understanding what it means and how to apply it to our daily lives.

My intent in this book is to challenge your current mental models and thinking biases. I do not expect you to believe what I have written without confirming my words with your own study of the scriptures. In fact, I challenge you to go to the Word and discover in your own study, inspired by the Holy Spirit, the evidence for a transformed life in Jesus Christ. See if you have a clear biblical understanding of how you started out your life. You were born with the nature of Adam in his image. You sinned because it was your nature to do so. Even when you try to be good, there is no way for any of us to be good enough in our behavior to compensate for our sinful nature. This is why Jesus had to die on the cross for us. We cannot save ourselves by our own actions no matter how good they might seem. I have witnessed a unique irony in the spiritual transformation of most people. Before they come to Christ they are so focused on doing "good things" and behaving well. Then they come to Christ and develop a false sense of security that how they choose to behave no longer has any consequences. Paul addressed this in his letter to the Romans: your works cannot save you and you should not sin so that grace might abound.

God had a plan for our redemption from the fallen nature of Adam. He loves us so much that He chose to offer Himself as a sacrifice. Is there any way we can fathom the depth of that kind of love? I don't think so. I served as a career military officer, and I know of soldiers who gave of themselves, their very lives, for the sake of their comrades in arms. I can relate to that level of self-sacrifice for those whom you love. The Bible says that while we were yet sinners, at war with God, He gave Himself for us so that we could be reconciled to Him. That is a love that is beyond my comprehension – loving me at my worst. Loving me when I choose to reject Him, yet He just keeps right on loving me and calling me to Himself.

Not only does He plan for me to be redeemed, He creates the way for me to be restored, transformed, and ultimately conformed into the image of His original creation. By entering into Jesus Christ, abiding and putting my life in Christ, I am set free from the bondage and burden of my Adam nature to live in the freedom of my reborn life in Christ. There is no condemnation for me in Jesus. Not only is there no condemnation, there is no expectation of having to earn His love. No performance measure for His love. His love is unconditional.

I told you in the beginning of this book that I am praying for you. Well I still am praying for you. Satan is not going to want you to know the truth. The Bible says you shall know the truth, and the truth shall set you free. So many people have bad thinking trapped in their hearts and minds. There is so much baggage of false thinking that they have acquired throughout their lifetimes. "You don't understand," they will tell me. "I can't change," they will tell me. People are living with burdened hearts and burdened souls, and they are living in self-imposed spiritual poverty to the point they will even begin to doubt their own salvation. These people are trapped in their emotions and feelings rather than relying on the truth of God's Word.

Are you one of these people? If so, I have good news for you - great news for you. You can be healed and set free. All you need to do is have a tool and a framework to renew your mind and begin to walk in the truth of God's Word in your life. It will be hard at first – all change is hard even change we want and know we need in our lives. The first step is to have a willing and submitted heart that is surrendered to Jesus. Then you need to be convinced in your mind that God's Word is truth and all other thoughts and beliefs are lies. You need to walk in the light of God's Word and not in the teaching and philosophy of this world. You need to allow the Holy Spirit to lead and guide you. You need to be compelled by the power of the Holy Spirit in your life. You cannot do in your flesh what God has already done for you in the Spirit. Then and only then, can you finally enter into His grace and peace and walk in a transformed life conforming to the image of His Son. A simple prayer can begin this process for you.

Father God I know that I have lived a life in confusion and turmoil. My heart is heavy and I am unsure of your love for me. Help me in my unbelief. I acknowledge my sin nature and confess my sins to you. I ask to receive your free gift of salvation through your Son, Jesus. I need you to heal my mind of years of bad thinking and false beliefs. Set me free to walk in the truth of your Word. Fill me with the overflowing power of the Holy Spirit and complete your work that you have begun in my life to conform me to the image of your Son.

Your heavenly Father desires that you live your life in the joy of the Spirit. Beyond our personal joy, we are to be an example to others. I know the Bible says that in this world we will have tribulations and trials. I am not talking in a Polly Anna mindset to you. Tragedy and troubles can come to us all in this world, but we have the promise that all things work to our good because we live in Christ Jesus. Our joy and our hopes are in Jesus. You must understand that the outcome of our spiritual warfare has already been decided – we have won. You are not fighting a battle to win the war. In reality, the war is over. That is why you can have joy even though the battle is still raging. Do not allow the trials and difficulties of this world to rob you of your joy, peace, and your victory in Jesus Christ. Nothing can separate us from the love of God. Everything about who we are in Christ begins and ends in His unconditional love. We have our joy in His love, and we have our victory in His love. Jesus says come to me you who are weary and heavy laden, and I will give you rest. My prayer for you is that you will believe in your heart, live with truth in your renewed mind, be compelled by the Holy Spirit, and be conformed into the image of the Son of God who loves you more than you ever will be able to imagine.

May the Lord bless you and keep you. May the Lord be attentive to you and grant you His peace.

Michael

Acknowledgements

I am blessed to have the love and support of an awesome wife, Susan. I want to thank her for her faithfulness in her walk with God and the example of faith she has been to me throughout our marriage. I owe her more than I can ever repay in her devotion to God and to our family.

I am blessed to be surrounded by a wonderful congregation. The love of these people sustains me as a pastor and challenges me to give more of myself in service to the ministry that God has given to us at Calvary Chapel Northeast Columbia. I am humbled and privileged to serve such a loving group of people who are committed to growing in their faith, learning the truth of God's Word, and applying it in their lives every day.

There have been some people who have helped me in the writing and publishing of this book. I know that you share in the hope of the lives that will be changed from reading what you have contributed in this finished work. To my wife, Susan, for letting me read and share the ideas that shaped the main contents. To several folks who assisted in proof-reading for me to eliminate the typographical and grammatical errors: Becky Frisina, Laurie Moore, Ginny Sohm, Carl Naso, and Dave Moyle. I give my thanks to Michael Caryl and the wonderful folks at Xuolon Press. Thank you for being so patient and professional in the printing and promotional work on this project. I accept responsibility for any errors and I want to give full credit to references cited to the original work of others that helped me put my own thoughts into this book. I do not make any claim to original thinking in this book, but only that I tried to write from my heart with the hope of it influencing change in your own thinking, so that you can be conformed to the image of Jesus Christ.

Consequently, I want to thank you, the reader. My prayer is that you would read the Holy Bible and grow in your knowledge and wisdom of the Word of God. I pray for the renewing of your mind daily, and that you would present yourself as a living sacri-fice to God and surrender to His plan and purpose for your life. This really is the only way to live an abun-dant life in Jesus Christ. This is really the only way to find the peace we all so desperately desire from the cares and worries of this world. Come to me Jesus says, and I will give you rest. What are you waiting for - go to Him today and may God richly bless you in the grace and peace of His unending love.

References

Peter Senge, *The Fifth Discipline* (New York: Doubleday Currency, 1990).

See http://www.butterflybushes.com/monarch_meta-morphosis.htm.

See http://www.crystalinks.com/12laborshercules.html.

Adam Nelson, "What Really Moves People: How Learning Changes Employees," *Chief Learning Officer* (May 2008):34-38.

Daniel Goleman, *Primal Leadership: Learning to Lead with Emotional Intelligence* (Boston: Harvard Business School Press, 2002).

Robert K. Cooper. *Get Out of Your Own Way* (New York: Crown Business, 2006).

The Speaker's Quote Book: Over 4,500 Illustrations and Quotations. Google Books Result by Roy B. Zook, 448.

Indiana Jones and the Last Crusade. Director, Stephen Spielberg. Videocassette. Paramount, 1999.

Bill Capodagli and Lynn Jackson, *The Disney Way* (New York: McGraw-Hill, 2002).

Tim Kight, *The R-Factor,* (Dublin, Ohio: Focus3, 2007).

Marshall Goldsmith, *What Got You Here Won't Get You There*, (New York: Hyperion, 2007).

Kerry Patterson, et.al, *Influencer*, (New York: McGraw-Hill, 2008).

<a href="http://sports.jrank.org/pages/2901 Lombardi-Vince.html">Vince Lombardi Biography - The Early Years, First Coaching Position, College Football, Chronology, Awards And Accomplishments, Moving Up With The Giants</a>

C.S. Lewis, *Mere Christianity: What One Must Believe to Be a Christian.* (New York: Macmillan Publishing. 1978).

J.C. Ortiz, *Living With Jesus Today.* (London: Triangle Books. 1984).

Adrian Rogers, *The Marks of a Christian*, retrieved July 1, 2008, http://www.oneplace.com/ ministries/Love_Worth_Finding/Article_ Archives.asp

Printed in the United States
136583LV00001B/1/P